HARNESS THE
BUSINESS WRITING PROCESS

THIRD EDITION

E-mail – Letters – Proposals – Reports
Media Releases – Web Content

PAUL LIMA

www.paullima.com/books

Cover and interior design, Paul Lima

Published by Paul Lima, Toronto, Ontario, Canada
www.paullima.com/books

First Edition copyright © 2009 by Paul Lima
Second Edition copyright © 2010 by Paul Lima
Third Edition (beta) copyright © 2011 by Paul Lima.

Quantity discounts available for instructors and workshop leaders
purchasing class sets. Contact Paul Lima - info@paullima.com.

Library and Archives Canada Cataloguing in Publication
Lima, Paul, 1954-

Harness the Business Writing Process / Paul Lima. – 3rd edition.
ISBN 978-0-9809869-2-1

1. Business writing. 2. English language—Business English.
I. Title.

Table of Contents

Preface

Welcome to *Harness the Business Writing Process*, a book written specifically for those who want to improve their business-writing skills, including their e-mail, letter, proposal, report, media release, and Web-writing ability.

This book is based on a business-writing course that I teach online for University of Toronto continuing education students and for private students and corporate clients. *Harness the Business Writing Process* is for you if you are looking to

- become a more effective writer;
- become a more efficient writer;
- organize your thoughts before you write;
- make your points in a clear, concise, focused manner;
- get your readers to take clearly defined actions;
- achieve your purpose.

In all honesty, this book is not for you if you want to learn the rules of grammar or learn how to spell better. This book will help you write in a more focused and concise manner, and it will help you simplify your written communication, which should help you improve your grammar on one level. However, this is not a grammar book. There are many grammar books out there. This book is all about communicating more effectively—conveying your purpose in a concise and focused manner so your readers understand why you are writing and what action you need them to take—whether you are writing a short e-mail message or a much longer and more sophisticated report.

When it comes to business writing, this book will get you grounded and focused—especially if you feel like you're often spinning your wheels when you write. *Harness the Business Writing Process* will get you thinking about your audience, your purpose, and your desired outcome before you start to write. Then it will help you effectively and efficiently write well-structured, focused documents in a clear, concise manner. You will be introduced to the business-writing process and come to understand the importance of following that process no matter what you are writing. Exercises in this book will help you apply the writing process to e-mail messages, letters, proposals, reports, media releases, and Web copy.

Although this is a business-writing book, it is my hope that you will have some fun as you push your writing to the point where you are communicating in an effective, professional, and business-like manner. Unlike many writing books, this one makes no promises of instant success. Writing is a process. To improve your writing, you need to understand the process and apply it in a dedicated and disciplined manner.

I hope to inspire you, give you options to pursue, and create a solid foundation you can build on (or *upon which you can build*, you might write if your internal editor is a strict disciplinarian who insists that your writing must conform to all the standards espoused by your grade five schoolteacher).

Note: This is the third edition of the book. Unfortunately, there were formatting problems with the second edition. I revised a number of passages while fixing the formatting errors. This edition of the book should be 99.9% error-free. If you like to play "spot the typos," feel free to let me know if you find any, or have any other comments about the book.

E-mail me—info@paullima.com.

Paul Lima
www.paullima.com

Chapter 1: Communication Process

Communication is a process. If you want to communicate effectively—in writing or when speaking—you should understand the process. Communication requires a sender who sends a message through a channel to a receiver. The process is not complete, however, without feedback; feedback closes the communication loop. Sometimes, noise (competing messages, distractions, misunderstandings) interferes with your message; feedback lets you know if the receiver understood your message.

When you communicate in person, you can ask for feedback: ask people if they understood or have any questions. However, when you communicate in writing or other one-way media (such as broadcast), it is more difficult to ask for feedback. Advertisers have learned how to use direct- response marketing techniques such as discount coupons, time-limited offers, and so on to motivate and measure feedback.

Advertisers want feedback when they communicate so they can measure the effectiveness of promotions. If they don't know how effective promotional campaigns are, how will they know whether they should run the same ads again, modify them, or scrap them and come up with something new? In business writing, if you do not close the communication loop, how will you know if the desired action has been or will be taken?

Does closing the communication loop mean asking for replies from everybody you e-mail or to whom you send information? Not necessarily. In many instances, your writing purpose might not require you to close the loop. You might simply be sending information for the recipient to review

—no action required. Or you might be making suggestions or recommendations that the recipient can to act on or ignore.

In other instances, however, you might have to know if the recipient has taken action or has any questions. If so, you need to close the communication loop. You can ask for a reply, you can send a reminder e-mail or follow-up by phone, or you can monitor the situation to see if action has been taken. Again, if you do not require a reply, then you may not need to close the communication loop. Deciding whether to close it or not should be a conscious decision, however, based on your particular business needs.

For instance, if you don't care who shows up, or how many people show up, to a meeting, then there is no reason to ask people to reply. But if you need to know how many people will be coming to the meeting so you can arrange lunch, then you had better ask people to let you know if they can attend. Do you have to give the caterer two days' notice to arrange lunch? Then you had better ask people to reply several days before the meeting.

The important point: if you need to know that the receiver has received and understood your message, then you have to put into place a method of closing the communication loop. If the loop does not close in a timely manner—timely as dictated by you and your circumstances—then it is your job to troubleshoot the process. In other words, you can assume that your message has been received and understood or you can build feedback into the communication process. With that in mind, we will look at ways to clearly communicate any required action to recipients of your documents.

It may seem odd to start a book on business writing with obtaining feedback. However, you communicate in writing for a reason that usually involves a required, or optional, action. In other words, if you do not know your reason for communicating, if you do not spell out the action you want taken, and if you do not close the communication loop, then you might not achieve your purpose. Or you might achieve your purpose and not know it because you have not asked the reader to close the communication loop.

With that in mind, where do we begin? How do we tackle business writing? I suggest we begin at the beginning, with the business-writing process—a process that can be applied to any non-fiction writing, even essays, articles, theses, and other documents not generally associated with business writing. But our focus here will be on business writing.

Chapter 2: Pleased to Meet You

Just as there is a communication process, there is also a writing process. It is a different kind of process. It is the approach you should take before you write, as you are writing, and once you have completed writing a document.

If you follow the process, you will become a more effective writer. It's that simple.

You will also become a more efficient writer if you practice following the process. However, as you read the first part of this book, you might find yourself thinking that if you have to go through the entire process every time you write something, it will take you forever to write anything.

Allow me to ask you this: Would you rather take a little longer to write a document that achieves what you want to achieve, or take less time and not achieve your purpose? I presume you would rather do the former. If you do not achieve your purpose when you communicate, you will end up spending more time sorting out problems or issues caused by miscommunication or ineffective communication.

Most people who follow the writing process find they become more effective *and* efficient writers. It takes process-practice to become a more efficient writer; however, following the process will make you a more effective writer from the start. Being a more effective writer will save you time when it comes to sorting out business issues; practicing the writing process will make you a more efficient writer too.

If you mostly write short e-mail messages, you may feel skeptical about my "efficiency" claim as you read the first few chapters of this book. Please be patient and wait until you come to the five-question writing process shortcut (W5) for writing e-mail messages and other short documents. Again, though, even if following the writing process adds a bit of time to the time it takes you to produce documents, you will become someone who can clearly convey your purpose and desired action so that your readers understand why you are writing and what you expect them to do. I suspect that is something to which every business writer aspires.

First introduction

Before you read about the writing process, I want you to take a moment and pretend you are introducing yourself to me. As you will see, I want you to write your introduction three times. To start, I simply want you to write the first introduction however you feel like writing it. Take some time now, before you read on, and write your introduction. I will explain how to write introductions two and three shortly.

Once you have written your first introduction, continue to read.

Writing process overview

Before you write your introduction a second and third time, allow me to introduce you to the foundation of this book—the writing process. The writing process includes five steps. Although all five steps involve writing, in terms of pen on paper or fingers on keyboard, only one step is writing as we view it in the conventional sense of word—constructing sentences and paragraphs. With that in mind, here are the five steps that make up the writing process:

- Preparation
- Research
- Organization
- Writing
- Revision

Again, notice that writing is only one of the steps in the writing process. We will, of course, examine each of these steps in detail. For now, however, I want to focus on why writing is a process and why, when writing, you should take the five steps in order.

If you are like me, you fear the blank screen or blank page. You look at it and feel intimidated. You see it as an empty vessel you have to fill with words—only you are not quite sure which words to use, how to order them, or how to use all those squiggles (known as punctuation marks).

Perhaps you are not like me. Perhaps you love the sight of a blank page. You view it as a blank canvas, an opportunity to create. However, you may feel your creations take too long to come to fruition. You start, you stop, you start again. Moving forward is a slow, painful journey, and you often feel you've missed your mark or destination, even if just by a tad, when you are done.

Welcome to the wonderful world of writing.

Writing seems to be painful in some way for almost everyone. For instance, when it comes to spelling and grammar, English is a convoluted and inconsistent language. For many of us, including me, spelling and grammar—let alone stringing words together in coherent sentences—can be frustrating. If you're my age, that frustration might include some early memories of grade school teachers who seemed to relish slashing thick red marks through your earnest writing efforts. As confusing as the rules are, having a teacher crush your work under the weight of red slashes can make the act of writing itself an intimidating endeavor.

You can improve your writing, however, and you can write better in less time than it takes you to complete a document today. All you have to do is harness the writing process, which we will discuss in detail in Chapter 4.

Second introduction

I now want you to write your second introduction. This time, we are going to prepare using who, what, where, when, and why, known as the W5. Before we look at how you would apply the W5, however, let's look at a few of the things you need to know before you begin to write almost any document:

- Word count or page length
- Due date
- Audience and audience's expectations
- Purpose or objective

We know this version of your introduction is due before you complete this chapter, since I am asking you to do it now. You can pretend you are going to send it to me to show me a sample of your writing and to introduce yourself to me. Since it is an introduction, not a book or a report, it should not be too long.

As your reader or audience, what do you think I need from you? In other words, what is my expectation? Do I want your life history, or do I simply want to know who you are and what you do in relation to why you purchased this book? Although the former might be an interesting read, will it be a practical read? The latter, on the other hand, is what you might expect me to want to know.

Finally, what is your purpose in writing your introduction? Let's assume you want to tell me why you bought the book and what you hope to get out of it—how you hope it might help you. With that in mind, I want your second introduction to answer the following questions:

- *Who* are you?
- *What* do you do (or hope to do)?
- *Where* did you buy this book?
- *When* did you decide to buy this book?
- *Why* did you decide to buy this book?

Before you write your introduction, answer the above questions in point form. Then review your points and determine which ones you'd want to use in your introduction. How do you determine that? Think of who I am and who you are, my (the reader's) expectations, and your purpose for writing. Eliminate any points that don't make the cut, write your second introduction, and revise it as may be required.

Once you have written your second introduction, continue to read.

What did we do?

Consider the writing of your second introduction as an introduction to the writing process. How so? Let's look at what we just did:

1. Preparation
   a. Defined the audience
   b. Determined the expectations of the reader
   c. Defined the writer's purpose
2. Research
   a. Conducted internal research by answering the W5 questions
3. Organization

   a. Organized the document into a rudimentary outline (when you eliminated points you did not want to cover)
4. Writing (first draft)
5. Revision

The preparation, research, and organization should have helped you focus your document on your reader and your purpose, as well as eliminate any points that did not relate to your reader or purpose. Therefore, you should have a more focused and concise document that makes sense to the reader and helps you achieve your purpose. Shouldn't any business document be both focused and concise? Shouldn't it make sense to the reader and help the writer achieve a predefined purpose?

Third Introduction

So are we done introducing? Maybe. It depends on two things: how long is your introduction and what person did you use? Did you use first person (I, me, my, we, us) or third person (he, she, they)? While business correspondence can be in first person, it is often in third person. You could write a message like this: "Based on our second quarter sales, I have decided to give all of my employees a bonus." You are more likely, however, to write a message like this: "Based on second quarter sales, ABC Inc. has decided to give all employees a bonus."

Sometimes the choice of which person to use is subjective. For instance, I have chosen to use third person on my website (www.paullima.com) to promote my business writing and business-writing training:

> Business writer and business-writing trainer Paul Lima can deliver the right words, on time and on budget, or train your staff to write more effectively. Based in Toronto, Paul has been a freelance writer, copywriter, and business-writing instructor for over 25 years. He offers companies and organizations a variety of business writing and copywriting services and business-writing training services.

The above statement feels credible; it does not feel like hard sell copy or content. Again, that may be a subjective interpretation. However, the distance of third person can lend objectivity and a greater degree of credibility to a document, as in this case:

> After reviewing the results of the recent product awareness survey, ABC Consulting recommends that 123 Ltd. broaden its marketing reach to include adults between the ages of 35 and 45.

By using "ABC Consulting," the document carries more weight. In other words, the company—not just one individual—is making, and therefore standing behind, this recommendation. Replace "ABC Consulting Inc." with "I" and the statement loses power.

In addition, bios are often written in third person—perhaps to appear on a website or to be read by someone who introduces you before you make a presentation or give a speech. Third person also gives you a sense of distance from yourself. That sense of distance can help you revise your work to ensure it is as focused, complete, and concise as it should be.

There are times when using first person is perfectly acceptable and even preferable. For now, though, I want you to review your second introduction. If it uses first person, I want you to write it one more time, in third person. Even if your bio is already in third person, make sure the length is appropriate for the occasion. Remember, you were asked to introduce yourself to the author of this book. Ask yourself what the author would want to know about you, the buyer of the book, and what you would want the author to know. If your bio is more than five sentences long, reduce it to no more than five sentences. In this way, you will more formally experience revision, the final step in the writing process.

Once you have written your third introduction, continue to read. If you want to introduce yourself to me, feel free to email your introduction to info@paullima.com.

Chapter 3: Loosening Up

Before we look at more formal aspects of business writing, I want to introduce you to two writing exercises—freefall and directed freefall—that will help you separate the writer from the editor. The writer is your creative self and exists in the right side of your brain. The editor is your logical or linear self and exists in the left side of the brain. Your goal should be to write or create first, and then revise later. In other words, when writing, you want to keep the left and right sides of your brain separated.

Internal critic

We all have an internal critic harping at us to get our writing right. At the same time, it's just so darned difficult to remember all the picayune and inconsistent rules of English.

My internal critic is Mr. C, my grade five teacher. Mr. C took his task of teaching me perfect spelling and grammar seriously by wielding his red marker like the sword of Zorro, forcefully cutting huge red gashes across my mistakes. He never once commented on content or creativity. To him, writing was all about correct spelling and grammar, as well as neatness or penmanship.

In grade five, students were supposed to graduate from pencil to pen during the year—as their spelling, grammar, and penmanship improved. But Mr. C made me use a pencil all year because I could not spell well or write neatly. I only received my pen on the last day of class. Mr. C tossed it at me and said, "Here, Lima, you'll need this next year. Good luck!"

But look at the language I was trying to master! Is it *i* before *e* (or *e* before *i*) except after, or before, *c*? How do you spell *weird*? That word is just, well, plain weird. In other words, even if you got the rules right, there were exceptions to almost every rule.

Of course, Mr. C was right. My writing was messy. For whatever reason, I could not remember most of the rules, and when I did manage to remember some of them, I could not remember the exceptions.

When you can't spell well, you try to hide the fact, which is why my penmanship was so poor. For instance, when you don't know if it's *i* before *e*, you make a chubby *i* and a skinny *e* and put the dot right in the middle and hope to fool the teacher!

Bottom line, I was a poor speller who did not punctuate very well. And my penmanship was abysmal. By the way, if you think that you cannot start a sentence with *and* or any other conjunction, you are wrong. But you probably learned that you could not do so from a grade school English teacher.

I don't want to say they lied to you, but they did. I would never suggest that you start most sentences with conjunctions such as *and, but,* or *because.* Because that can make your writing a tad awkward to read. And people who believe you cannot start a sentence with a conjunction might think you have made a mistake. There could be times, however, when starting a sentence with a conjunction might help you focus on a particular point in the message you are trying to convey. So keep this tip in mind. But use it sparingly.

Battling Mr. C

I battle Mr. C when I attempt to master the art and craft of writing—even when writing business documents. Today, however, when he rears his fearsome head, I say, "Get thee behind me!" And I keep on writing through typos and grammatical errors. Through incomplete sentences and incorrect words. I write until I have finished an error-filled first draft, and then I laugh in his face. Because I have learned that *writing is a process.*

If you look at the process, you will see that in the first step, you prepare to write. Then you conduct your research—internal and/or external, depending on the scope of the project, your readers' expectations, and your knowledge or mastery of the topic. Then you get organized. Only then do you write. And while you are writing, you do not need to revise, edit, or proofread.

In other words, it is okay to make mistakes when you write because the process allows you to correct them when you finish your first draft. After all, your first draft is for your eyes only, so who cares if it contains spelling or grammatical mistakes that you can correct before you send it out for review, for approval, or to be read by your audience?

If you do not follow the process, Mr. C will trip you up every time. He will get you revising and editing when you should be creating. He will cause you to waste time proofreading work that is not even at the first draft stage. He will have you feeling inadequate because you are planning instead of actually writing something—as if it were illegal, immoral, or unethical to think before you write. In short, if you allow your internal critic to dominate you, you will feel frustrated and your writing will suffer.

Words for thought

Writing is difficult enough without having your internal critic squeeze the last ounce of fun out of what should be a challenging but enjoyable and creative art or craft. With that in mind, chew on a few words for thought:

> It took me my whole life to learn how to paint like a child again.
> - *Pablo Picasso*

◨   ◨   ◨

> Never look at a reference book while doing a first draft. You want to write a story? Fine. Put away your dictionary, your encyclopedias, your World Almanac and your thesaurus.... You think you might have misspelled a word? Okay, so here's your choice: either look it up in the dictionary to make sure you have it right—and break your train of thought—or spell it phonetically and correct it later. Why not? Do you think the word is going to go away? When you sit down to write, write. Don't do anything else except go to the bathroom and only do that if it absolutely cannot be put off.
> - *Stephen King, On Writing: A Memoir of the Craft*

◨   ◨   ◨

So what are King and Picasso saying? When you are writing (painting or engaged in any creative art or craft), you must overcome your inhibitions and internal censors. In short, when you are writing, spelling and grammar do not count. Spelling and grammar are important; however, there will be time for correcting later, once you plan your attack and complete your first draft, which is for your eyes only. Who cares if there are typos? Fix them later.

If you are working in a word processing program such as Word and you have your spell checker and grammar checker turned on, you are inviting your Mr. C to inhibit your writing. The green and red squiggles under your words, phrases, and sentences mean you are seeing (and correcting) so-called mistakes as you write—before you complete your first draft. Every time you revise—when you should be writing—you are wasting time and derailing your train of thought. If you want to improve your writing productivity immediately, turn off spell check and grammar check. Write when you should write; edit/proofread after you have written.

I want to reinforce one point before we move on. *Spelling and grammar are important.* I try my darnedest to catch spelling and grammar mistakes. However, I don't do it while I am writing my first draft. I do it after I have completed what I consider a solid first draft. In fact, before I look for spelling and grammatical mistakes, I edit for big picture items such as tone and content. Then I focus on the more mundane—yet important—task of checking spelling and grammar.

Freefall

Having said all that, I know it can be difficult to separate your editor from your writer. That's why I want to introduce you to freefall writing, also known as stream of consciousness writing.

Freefall is a means of writing whereby you literally write, for five minutes or so, without stopping. When you freefall, you don't have to have anything in particular to write about. You just put pen to paper (recommended over fingers to keyboard) and write, write, write. You don't stop, no matter what. Think of yourself as an artist practicing gesture sketching (rapidly drawing and playing with lines or "gestures" that do not necessarily become pictures).

To sustain your freefall, tap into your stream of consciousness—the thoughts that are flowing through your mind (even as you are reading this page, you can hear them rushing through your mind)—and write, write, write. If you feel yourself coming to a halt, doodle or use ellipsis (...) until you tap back into the stream. Do not stop.

Do not stop to correct spelling, grammar, or punctuation.

Do not stop to reflect upon or edit your work.

Do not stop.

It can feel unusual to write when you think you have nothing to say, or to continue to write when you know you have made a spelling or grammatical error. However, that is the whole point—to get used to the separation of writer and editor by jumping into the stream and letting the current take you somewhere, anywhere, or nowhere in particular.

As you will see, freefall is a technique that I will encourage you to employ after you have completed your preparation, research, and organization, and before you revise. Writing this way can take a bit of getting used to, although you will probably take to it like a fish to water (or any other cliché you can think of when you are freefalling and the perfect analogy does not come immediately to mind).

Let's freefall

I want to stress here that your freefall does not have to be a straight narrative. Have fun. Play. Experiment. Push your personal boundaries. If you latch on to something that feels like a bit of business writing or work-related writing, run with it. But do not try to impose form or narrative on your freefall. Write fast. Do not pause. Especially do not pause to revise.

What I suggest that you do now is this:

- Sit comfortably where you will not be interrupted for the next while.
- Write for at least five minutes; if you can, set a timer for five minutes.
- Pick up your pen, start with whatever is flowing through our mind, and keep on going.
- Don't stop until your time is up.

If you are not ready to freefall, take a break. But don't put off starting for too long. When you are ready…

…*Begin your freefall.*

Once you have written a five-minute freefall, continue to read.

Freefall purpose

Now that you've done your first freefall, you may well be thinking, "Is there a purpose to it?"

Is there a point or purpose to all the gesture sketches an artist does, the voice exercises an opera singer does, or the stretching a runner does? This is your warm-up. This is you getting in shape. This is you learning to write for the sake of writing. This is you in a no-pressure, not-for-publication situation discovering the joy of writing—even if it feels like a pain. This is you separating the writer from the editor. This is you learning how to become a more efficient and effective writer.

I encourage you to do this exercise daily to help you loosen up and write quickly. You might even want to freefall before you start reading each chapter. However, since you are new to freefall, please try one more—before you read on. Get comfortable, set your timer and...

...Begin your freefall.

Once you have written your second freefall, continue to read.

Directed freefall

Directed freefall works in a manner similar to freefall, but you start with an opening line—something to help kick-start your writing. Once you start, you carry on writing just as with freefall.

You can find directed freefall "beginnings" or opening lines almost anywhere: a sentence in a newspaper, book, or report; a snippet of overheard conversation; something you hear on the radio; something you read on the Web; and so on.

The opening line sometimes imposes structure on your writing or leads to you writing a narrative passage. But not always. Sometimes it inspires. But not always. Sometimes it is a relief to have somewhere to start. Sometimes it makes you feel shackled. The point is to use the first line as a starting point and freefall, no matter how you feel.

So take five minutes or so, and try a directed freefall using the line below. If you are not ready to freefall, take a break. But don't put off starting for too long. When you are ready...

...Begin your directed freefall starting with the following line:

It took a long time to...

Once you have written a five-minute directed freefall, continue to read.

When you have completed your directed freefall, try several other lines. Look for lines of your own to get started, or you can use any of these:

- *I find it frustrating when...*
- *If I've told you once, I've told you a thousand times...*
- *Terry had to reschedule the meeting because...*

The goal is to have fun, to play, to create for the sake of creating. To write without revising because separating the writer from the editor is an important part of the writing process. Off the top, it makes you a more efficient writer if you work diligently at keeping the writer and editor separate. Also, as you will see when we get to creating outlines, directed freefall—starting to write with an opening line—is an integral part of becoming a more effective business writer.

Again, as you read this book, freefall regularly. Freefall (or use directed freefall) at different times of the day. Eventually, you might settle into a best time to freefall. The important thing is that you make five minutes or so every day to freefall.

Once you have written your second directed freefall, continue to read.

Chapter 4: Writing Process

As indicated in Chapter 2, there are five steps in the writing process:
1. Preparation
2. Research
3. Organization
4. Writing
5. Revision

The time required to complete each step varies depending on the nature of the project. For instance, if you are a subject matter expert, you might not have to spend any time on external research. If you write a particular type of document regularly, you might not have to spend much time on preparation; you might even have a template you fill in each time you write.

When writing a short e-mail message, you can prepare, research, and organize by answering a few simple questions that I will address later. Answers to these questions will help you think about your audience and purpose and generate the points (organization) you want to cover in your message. Once you have put your list of points in order, writing should be as simple as turning the points into sentences. Then you revise to ensure you are making your primary point (conveying your purpose), proofread to check spelling and grammar, and send.

When writing a formal report, however, you will spend much more time preparing, researching, and organizing. You might even have to produce a formal outline (an integral component of organization) for approval before you start to write. As you write, section by section, you might discover gaps in your knowledge and have to conduct more research and incorporate new material into your outline. When you complete your first draft, you will probably spend considerable time revising to ensure that your writing is as clear, concise, and focused as it can be, and that all points covered in the report reinforce your purpose and conclusion or any recommendations that you have made.

You might have to send your document to a superior or a committee for approval. Your superior or the committee will most likely make suggestions and send it back to you for additional work. That is to be expected and is all part of the process.

Effective and efficient

If you follow the writing process, you will become a more effective *and* efficient writer.

Efficient writers spend time planning (preparation, research, and organization) before they write. And they allocate time for editing (revising and proofreading). This leads to the writing of effective documents, documents that achieve a specific purpose.

Less efficient writers tend to spend more time overall on projects even though they spend less time planning. They also edit as they write, which is to say they write, tinker, write, revise, write, correct little errors, and so on. This is not a productive way to write and, because less efficient writers don't plan what they want to write, they end up with less satisfactory, or less effective, results.

It may seem ironic to say that you can become more efficient if you spend more time planning. However, the time you invest up front in preparation, research, and organization pays dividends when it comes time to write and revise.

Think of writing as a trip. If you plan your trip, you are less likely to get lost and more likely to arrive on time. That does not mean you cannot meander as you travel. You can. However, if you meander and your side trip takes you nowhere, you will find it easier to get back on track because you have a road map or, in the case of writing, a process that includes a detailed outline.

Writing process overview

With that in mind, let's briefly review each component of the five-step writing process. I will help you apply the most significant aspects of the major components as you work your way through this book.

As you read the next few chapters, remember that I will also soon show you a writing process shortcut for e-mail and other short documents. Before you get to the shortcut, however, you need to understand the full process.

Preparation

- Establish your primary purpose
- Assess your readers (or audience) and their expectations and awareness of the issue(s) about which you are writing
- Determine the detail into which you must go to achieve your purpose
- Select the appropriate medium for delivering your words

Research

- Determine if the research will be internal, external, or a combination of both
- Find appropriate sources of information
- Take notes and document external sources

Organization

- Select an appropriate method of development so that your writing unfolds in a logical manner
- Prepare an outline, breaking your document into manageable chunks
- Consider your layout, design, and visuals (illustrations, graphs, charts)

Writing

- Write from outline point to point, using each point like the opening line in a directed freefalls; expand each point into sentences and/or paragraphs
- Write with spell check and grammar check turned off
- Complete a first draft, or a full section of longer documents, before revising
- Write the introductions and conclusions of longer documents last

Revision

- Revise with the reader and subject matter in mind to ensure the tone is appropriate for both

- Revise to ensure your document is clear, concise, and focused and supports your purpose
- Check spelling and grammar
- Peer edit if possible

Know your audience

Later in the book, we will look at the importance of establishing, and how to establish, your primary purpose; we'll also talk a bit about determining the scope of your coverage (the detail into which you must go to achieve your primary purpose). For now, however, I want to take a brief look at this preparation point: *assess your readers (or audience) and their expectations and awareness of the issue(s) about which you are writing.*

In today's connected world, many companies span the globe. Even if you are working for a company that only does business in one country or one community, many countries and communities consist of multicultural societies. Your audience also may consist of different genders and people with different attitudes or educational levels. In short, unless you are writing to one person, it is rare that you will be writing for a homogeneous audience.

It is imperative that you know who the members of your audience are, and that you write to meet their business, cultural, and language expectations—all while writing to achieve your purpose.

Understanding your readers will help you determine your business writing style; the amount of research you conduct; the medium you select (paper report, website, e-mail, PDF file, and so on) to convey your message; the overall scope and tone of your document; and the content you choose to include and omit.

To help you think about your audience, before you begin to write, ask yourself:

What is the language skill level of my audience? If you are writing for an audience with a variety of language skills, ascertain the language skill of the most important stakeholders. If the language skills vary widely, keep your document as simple as possible or use glossaries and definitions to explain complex concepts and terminology.

What is the technical skill level of my audience? If you are writing a technical document for an audience with a wide range of technical skills or understanding, ascertain the technical knowledge of the most important stakeholders. If technical knowledge varies, keep your document as simple as possible. Include required technical details in appendixes, if they're appropriate to the medium, at the end of the document. Use glossaries and definitions to explain complex concepts and terminology.

What are my readers' expectations? Make sure you understand your readers' expectations, and how to react to them, before you begin to write. Are your readers expecting to be entertained or informed? Educated or sold? Coddled or persuaded? Should you meet those expectations or defy them for effect? Can you, should you, manipulate expectations?

What is the context in which the document will be received? You should know if you are writing to the converted or if you are writing for a skeptical audience—one with a number of built-in objections. This makes a difference to what you write, the detail you provide, and how you approach your topic in terms of tone, style, facts, and arguments.

Learning from advertisers

Advertisers get to know their target audience (or target market) intimately before they produce advertisements. They conduct research and produce ads that meet the expectations of a well-defined demographic (gender, age range, income level, education level, and so on). Sometimes they hold focus groups to get into the heads of their target market so they can produce ads that meet psychographic expectations. (Psychographics describe consumer groups based on psychological or emotional traits, characteristics, or lifestyles.)

While you may not need to know your audience as intimately as someone producing advertising or marketing material does, you can still learn from advertisers, in particular from the headlines they use to capture the attention of their target audiences.

Look at how the following headline clearly defines its target market:

Over 40? Acne Blemishes?

The headline is marketing an acne product for adults. Notice how it cuts through the clutter of all the other acne medication ads out there by clearly defining its target market: If you are under forty, then this ad is not for you;

if you are over forty but have a clear complexion, then this ad is not for you; if you are over forty and have acne, then this ad is for you.

The headline captures attention by clearly defining its target market and creating an expectation in the reader. The reader expects to find a solution to his or her acne problem.

If the rest of the ad copy does not quickly deliver on the implied promise of a solution (in other words, demonstrate how it will meet the created expectation) it will fail to hold the interest of the reader. If it does not hold the reader's interest, it cannot influence the reader's attitude—to believe the product will work, for instance. And if the ad does not influence the reader's attitude, it cannot motivate the reader into action—in this instance, to buy the product.

AIAA: attention, interest, attitude, action

You may not think you are *selling* when you write, but if you want your reader to take a specific action, you need to sell the reader. To do that, you need to do what advertisers do:

- **Attention**: Capture the attention of your reader and set expectations
- **Interest**: Hold reader's interest by demonstrating how you will meet relevant expectations
- **Attitude**: Change or influence your reader's attitude
- **Action**: Call for specific action

Depending on what you are writing, you AIAA, so to speak, by doing the following:

- Capture your reader's attention by using appropriate subject lines, titles and sub-titles, opening paragraphs, and/or executive summaries
- Hold your reader's interest with clear, concise, focused writing that reinforces the reader's beliefs and expectations, or enlightens the reader through the presentation of relevant information
- Influence or change your reader's attitude by overcoming any objections your reader might have, informing the reader of the benefits of your position, and by stating your case in a logical, persuasive manner—supporting your arguments with relevant facts

- Achieve your purpose by defining the action you want your reader to take and asking your reader to take it by a specific date

In summary, to be an effective business writer, you must AIAA so you can sell your purpose—the reason you are writing. Again, you may not believe that you are in sales, but if you want somebody to do something, you have to sell that person on the action you want taken.

The action might as complex as recommending a new highway be built or it might be something as simple as asking the reader to attend a meeting or send you a document. The point is, if you don't catch the person's attention, he will not read your message. If you don't hold the reader's interest, he will stop reading and not understand what you want done. If you don't influence attitude, the reader will not be motivated to do what you've requested. And if you do not clearly ask for the sale—or the action—you might not get what you want, when or where you want it.

In short, you are most likely reading this book because you want to become a more effective writer. The communication process, writing process, and AIAA are the foundation of effective writing.

Before we become more effective writers (and, I hope, more efficient ones too), however, we have to get organized. Let's start with a brainstorming technique known as clustering that will help you conduct internal research and will help facilitate the outlining or organizing process.

Chapter 5: Clustering/Brainstorming

I am now going to introduce you to a technique known as clustering, a form of word association or brainstorming. Clustering helps you conduct internal research—after you have completed any required external research—before you outline (organize) your document.

Clustering enables you to put on paper all you know about and associate with a topic. It helps you get your knowledge out in the open and helps you reduce the time you might otherwise spend pondering a topic. It also sparks writing ideas because, as you cluster, your mind makes associations and produces images that it would not have otherwise produced. These ideas and associations can help enrich your writing.

When clustering, you follow a specific process in which you quickly jot down all the words and phrases that you associate with a given topic, keyword, or phrase. Once you have completed the clustering process, you will find it much easier to produce a formal document outline; having a formal document outline helps you write in a more effective and efficient manner.

Since a picture is worth a thousand words, allow me to show you an example of clustering, on the next page, before I describe how to engage in this activity. What you see in the clustering illustration might look like a messy web of words and phrases. But it is also gold—internal research and outline gold. To organize your document, and to become a more effective and efficient writer, you just have to learn how to mine the gold from your clustering.

Be open to whatever comes up

When you engage in clustering, you produce words and phrases associated with your subject. You also may produce words and phrases that are only vaguely (or not at all) related. That's not a problem. Just as you do not censor yourself when you are freefalling, you do not censor yourself when you are clustering.

Sometimes jotting down unrelated words that may enter your mind when clustering can lead to jotting down related words and phrases. In other words, there are times when the mind moves in mysterious ways. Let it.

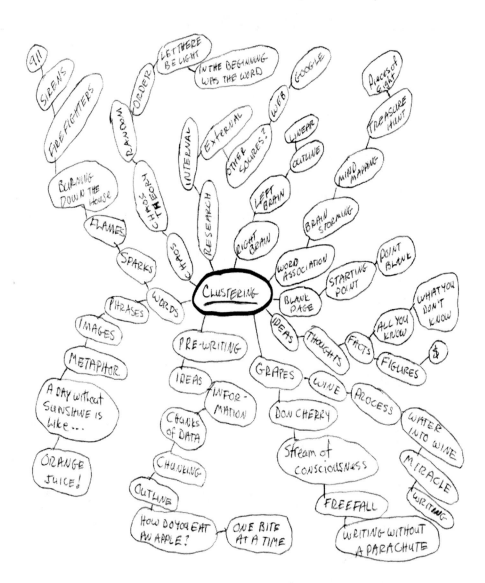

Clustering: how to do it

When clustering, you follow a specific process in which you quickly jot down all the words and phrases that you associate with a given topic, keyword, or phrase. Once you are given (or decide upon) your keyword or phrase, you follow these steps:

1. Jot down the keyword on a blank page; underline and circle it.
2. Moving quickly, draw a dash from your keyword and jot down the first word or phrase that comes to mind; circle that word or phrase.
3. Draw a dash from that word and jot down the next word or phrase that comes to mind.
4. Repeat until you come to the end of your word association string (you will feel this instinctively as you find yourself going blank).
5. Return to your keyword.
6. Moving quickly, draw a dash from your keyword and jot down the next word or phrase that comes to mind; circle that word or phrase.
7. Draw a dash from that word or phrase and jot down the next word or phrase that comes to mind; circle that word or phrase.
8. Follow the clustering process until you feel a natural end to your cluster. You may have on your page two or three strings of words; you may have twenty-two or more word association strings. There is no right or wrong number. The key is to move quickly using the lines and circles to help spark the creative side of your brain.

I generally find it easiest to use a pen and a piece of paper when I'm clustering, or perhaps a white board or flip chart if I'm brainstorming with a colleague or committee. On the other hand, if you are comfortable using computers, there are a number of clustering applications available: Inspiration is one of the more venerable "visual thinking" applications, but similar applications are available.

Clustering exercise

We'll look more closely at why we cluster, and how to use the results of clustering, in a moment. Right now, however, let's do it. Before you complete this first clustering exercise, read the above instructions again. Once you are ready, write down the keyword below and start to cluster. When you are ready, begin clustering using this keyword:

HEART

Once you have completed your cluster, continue to read.

Clustering exercise

Some people take to clustering right away. Some people find it difficult to cluster freely. Clustering is important and will prove to be particularly useful when you are writing longer documents. If you found it difficult, allow me to assure you that you will get better with practice. With that in mind, try one more clustering exercise.

Once you are ready, begin clustering using this keyword:

APPLE PIE

Once you have completed your cluster, continue to read.

Applying clustering

Do you have a sense of how clustering can help you conduct internal research or produce an outline? Perhaps not yet, as the above words may not mean all that much to you. In addition, I did not give you an assignment: you have no sense of audience or purpose. At this point, however, you should have two pages full of words or phrases that you associate with *heart* and *apple pie*.

Imagine if you were writing about *heart* or *apple pie* and that you had an audience and a purpose in mind. You would most likely have on paper all that you associated with *heart* and *apple pie* in relation to your audience and purpose. (You might also have words and phrases that don't quite relate to *heart* and *apple pie* or to your audience and purpose, but sometimes you have to jot down irrelevant information to get to the relevant material.)

If you had a purpose and audience in mind, and had completed your *heart* or *apple pie* research before you clustered, you could then review the word association strings you produced by clustering and separate the wheat from the chaff—literally highlight any words and phrases (topics) that you wanted to cover in your document. From that, as we shall see, you would produce your formal outline.

Before we find out if clustering works, allow me to quote an accountant who was taking a business-writing seminar in which I introduced clustering.

He had chosen to cluster a keyword that he associated with a major report he was writing for his firm. After completing his clustering, he said:

> You freed one gigabyte of RAM. I was holding it all in and you had me pull this information out of nowhere. Everything I need to know is down on paper. Now that I know what I'm going to say, I have brainpower left to think about how I'm going to say it. It's all over but the writing, and the writing is no longer intimidating.

He said this before moving from clustering to creating an outline. In other words, he saw in his spider's web of words everything he needed to write about and started to organize the information.

Clustering exercise

I know I said you should conduct your clustering after you had concluded any required external research; however, it does not hurt to use clustering as soon as you have a subject to write about because it can help you figure out what you know, and what you need to know, about the subject. Once you have completed your clustering, you do your research. Then, once you have completed your research, you cluster again to help you organize your thoughts. But I digress.

What I want you to do now is this: think of a keyword or phrase that you associate with an e-mail message, letter, report, research project, or other document that you are working on. (If you are not working on anything right now, think of a document that you have previously worked on.) Ideally, you want to pick a subject about which you have already conducted some research or about which you have extensive knowledge.

The keyword or phrase should be something that defines or summarizes the topic. Once you have that keyword or phrase in mind, write it down, underline it, circle it, and start clustering.

Once you are ready, begin clustering using this keyword:

<Your Keyword>

Once you have completed your cluster, continue to read.

What now?

Once you finish clustering, here's what you do:

- Take a highlighter to your web of words and highlight any words and phrases (topics) that you think you should write about in your document.

- Place the topic words or phrases in priority sequence (the order in which you think you should write about them) to produce a rough outline of your document.

- Review your draft outline and revise it as required based on your subject, purpose, and audience. Also keep in mind the scope of the document—short e-mail message versus a proposal or report, for instance. As you revise it, eliminate any points you don't need to cover and fill in any gaps with new points you might think of.

You don't have to do any more than that for now. In the next chapter, we will look at how to create a formal outline. However, I hope you can see how clustering can draw information out of you, and how producing an outline based on your clustering means that you don't have to start writing with a blank page. Instead, you can start with an outline, which is kind of like having a series of directed freefall opening lines. To write your document, you simply freefall from outline point to outline point. The more detailed your outline, the less you have to hold on to as you write, and the more effectively and efficiently you will be able to write.

By way of an aside, if, perhaps, you are looking for a job, you might want to use your name as the keyword. Clustering your name can help you to write your cover letter and résumé and help you prepare for interviews.

Chapter 6: Creating Outlines

Clustering is the first step in getting organized. The next step is to create an outline. Producing an outline before you write will help you write in a more effective and efficient manner.

To create an outline after clustering, you have to move from right-brain (creative) thinking to left-brain (linear) thinking.

After clustering, as I mentioned, take a highlighter to your spider's web of words and highlight any words and phrases that you want to write about in your document. Remember, at this point, you have already thought about your topic, audience, and purpose (we will examine purpose in detail later), so you should have a good sense of who you are writing for and why you are writing. Therefore, you can highlight words and phrases that relate to your subject matter, audience, and purpose.

Once you have highlighted appropriate words and phrases, you place them in a list to create a rough outline of your document. You review this list and revise it—put the topics in the order you think you should write about them. Again, this is based on your purpose, audience, and scope (the degree of detail expected by your audience or required to achieve your purpose). Also, you can consider your deliverable (e-mail, letter, report, PowerPoint presentation, and so on) you are producing

Review your ordered list and do some in-filling by adding any other topic points, or subtopic points, you feel may be missing. Remove any points that are not relevant, and you are almost there.

Why create an outline?

Does this feel like work? Most people think it does, and there is a valid reason for the feeling. It is work. But what's the alternative? You can, of course, try to fill the blank page with sentences that will make sense to your audience and help you achieve your purpose. But guess what happens when you try to do that? Your brain tries to write well—to write coherent, well-constructed sentences and paragraphs produced in a logical order—and to spell correctly and follow the rules of grammar. And, as it is trying to do all of that, it tries to keep track of what you have written, what you are writing, and what you still need to write.

Now your brain is a remarkable organ; it can do all of that, more or less. What I am suggesting you do here is relieve your brain of some of this workload by creating an outline—a formal list of all the points you need to cover placed in the order you feel you should write about them. An outline brings focus and logical order to your document. It liberates your brain and lets you concentrate on writing each point in a clear, concise manner. Your brain won't have to remember what you have written while thinking about what you are writing and what you still have to write. If you follow the writing process, which lists editing as the final component, you also free your brain from thinking about grammar and spelling on the first draft.

With all this liberated brainpower available to you, you can focus on making your writing as effective as possible. And isn't that your primary goal—to write as effectively as possible?

Creating outlines

Once you have your points on the screen in logical order, you convert them into more detailed points or even into sentences, and create your outline. Below are a couple of outline examples. The first is a major topic outline on the subject of creating outlines. The second is a more detailed outline on the same topic. The major topic outline includes the subject you are going to write about and, in this case, sets out the two major topics you are going to cover:

Creating outlines
1. How to create an outline
2. Benefits of outlining

To create a more detailed outline, you would add sub-points below the major topic headings, as in the following example:

Creating outlines
1. How to create an outline
   a. Outline major topic points
   b. Subdivide topic headings where appropriate

      i.   Further subdivide subcategories if appropriate

2. Benefits of outlining

   a. Provides logical structure

      i.   Helps you detect errors in logic

     ii.   Gives you a detailed road map

    iii.   Let's you meander, if you wish, without getting lost

   b. Removes the stress of trying to hold onto all you know about a topic while you are writing about it

      i.   Makes you a more confident writer

     ii.   Ensures all major and minor points are covered, in order

    iii.   Produces greater clarity and focus

   c. Allows you to write quickly in manageable chunks

      i.   Ensures you do not lose your train of thought when you have to take breaks from writing; give examples

   d. Facilitates the approval process, if approval is required

      i.   Lets you write from an approved outline

     ii.   *Should* minimize revisions by superiors

Benefits of outlines expanded

Can your outlines be even more detailed? Absolutely. The greater the scope of the document (in other words, the longer the document), the longer and more detailed the outline should be. I'll show you a longer outline shortly; however, first let me address some of the points listed under "Benefits of outlining" in the outline above.

Outlines provide a logical structure to your document. If you have brainstormed all the points you need to know and listed them in the order that you want to write about them, then you can detect errors in logic. I don't know about you, but I'd rather revise a series of outline points before I start to write than revise an entire report several times because my writing did not flow in a logical manner.

you have a detailed road map to follow, it will get you from point
oint B in the shortest possible time. Instead of weaving all over the
.ng road and heading down dead ends, you'll start where you should
.art, take the route you need to take, and end up where you want to be.
(Notice how that last sentence was not in my "benefits" outline. But notice
also how it is related to and logically follows the "gives you a detailed road
map" point. That is the kind of focused writing that an outline can help you
produce.)

Does that mean you cannot meander? Of course not. If you think of a
point that did not make it into your outline, you are free to explore it. If it is
something you should write about, make room in the outline for it. If it is
something that proves to be a dead-end, leave it out. The point is, even if
you wander, the outline will ensure that you don't get lost. It will keep you
on track, ensuring that you cover all major and minor points, in an order
that makes sense to you, to your topic, and to your reader.

A detailed outline means you do not have to hold on to all you know
about a topic while you are writing about it. That removes a great deal of
the stress that you might otherwise feel while you are writing and helps you
write with greater confidence. If you are covering all the major and minor
points you need to cover to convey your purpose or achieve your goal, then
you will write with greater clarity and focus.

With an outline in place, you can write quickly in manageable chunks.
Instead of having to write a fifteen-page report, you only have to write a
series of chunks or sections. That also reduces the stress associated with
writing. And it ensures you do not lose your train of thought when you
have to take breaks from writing. For instance, if the phone rings, you can
finish a sentence, take the call, and then pick up your writing at the next
outline point. Or you can go home at the end of the day knowing you will
come back to the document the next day and pick up where you left off—
because the next point you want to address is there in your outline.

If you have to get a major document approved before you can distribute
it, send the outline out for approval first. The person who has to approve
the document can see if you have covered in your outline all the points you
need to make. If any points are missing, or if the approver does not think
your points are as logically structured as they should be, then she can add
(or delete) points or move them around before sending the outline back to
you. When you start to write, you will be writing to an approved outline.

That does not mean the person who has to approve the report won't make some changes; however, the changes are more likely to be of a subjective nature rather than a request to revamp and reorganize your entire document. I know, however, that some people who have to approve documents will ask you to revamp or reorganize anything you've written, even if you have carefully followed the approved outline. That's why my last points said "*facilitates* the approval process" not "*guarantees* the approval" and "*should* minimize revisions by superiors" not "*will* minimize revisions…"

Even longer outlines

As I have said, if you are writing a long report or research paper or an academic thesis or book, you will want to produce a long, detailed outline. (If you are writing a non-fiction book, you might be interested in reading my book, *How to Write a Non-Fiction Book in 60 Days*.) I'd suggest that you divide your outline into major sections or chapters. Beyond that, the premise is the same: outline major and minor topic points. Be as detailed as possible because the time you invest up front, producing a detailed outline, will save you writing (and even revising) time.

In short, a section outline might look something like this:

Major topic of section (or chapter)
1. Major point 1
    a. Subpoint 1
    b. Subpoint 2
2. Major point 2
    a. Subpoint 1
    b. Subpoint 2
    c. Subpoint 3
    d. Subpoint 4
3. Major point 3
    a. Subpoint 1
    b. Subpoint 2

It is, however, recommended that you include secondary, tertiary, and other subpoints in your outline, such as this:

Major topic of section (or chapter)
1. Major point 1
   a. Subpoint 1
      i. Secondary point 1
      ii. Secondary point 2
         1. Tertiary point 1
         2. Tertiary point 2
   b. Subpoint 2
      i. Secondary point 1
         1. Tertiary point 1
         2. Tertiary point 2
      ii. Secondary point 2
         1. Tertiary point 1
         2. Tertiary point 2
         3. Tertiary point 3
   c. Subpoint 3
      i. Secondary point 1
      ii. Secondary point 2
         1. Tertiary point 1
         2. Tertiary point 2
         3. Tertiary point 3
2. Major point 2
   a. Subpoint 1
      i. Secondary point 1
         1. Tertiary point 1
         2. Tertiary point 2
   b. Subpoint 2
      i. Secondary point 1
         1. Tertiary point 1
         2. Tertiary point 2
   c. Subpoint 2
      i. Secondary point 1
         1. Tertiary point 1
         2. Tertiary point 2...

You keep on going until you have outlined every point in every section of your report (or in every chapter of your book). This presumes you have determined, in large part by using clustering and thinking about what your audience needs to know, the various sections of your report. In short, following the formal outline process will get you to the stage where it is all over but the writing from outline point to outline point. As any professional writer will tell you, that's a great place to be; however, you don't have to be a professional writer to get to that place.

Outlines in Word

From short e-mail messages to long reports, outlines are key to effective writing. Set up properly, they help you focus on all you have to write to meet the expectations of your readers and achieve your purpose. Acknowledging their importance, Microsoft Word and most other major word processing applications have outline views.

A detailed discussion about Word's outline view goes beyond the scope of this book; however, if you are not familiar with outline view, consider learning how to use it. Outline view lets you create a detailed outline. In addition, once you've completed your outline, you can move from outline view to print layout view and start writing from outline point to outline point.

Having said that, if you are not comfortable with Word's outline view, don't let the technology interfere with the creation of your initial outline. Use clustering to discover all the words and phrases you associate with your topic, and create your outline using pen and paper. Then transfer your outline into Word's outline view, if that works for you, or into a normal Word page view. Only when you are comfortable with the outline view set up, should you move directly from clustering to Word's outline view.

Clustering/outline exercise

Think of another word or phrase that you associate with an e-mail message, letter, report, research project, or other document that you are working on, or reuse the word or phrase you used in the last chapter. Once you have your word or phrase in mind, and are ready, begin clustering using

<Your Keyword>

Once you have completed your cluster, continue to read.

Now that you have completed your clustering, try to produce as detailed and formal an outline as possible based on the outline examples presented in this chapter. With that in mind, here's what you do:

- Take a highlighter to your web of words and highlight any words and phrases (topics) that you think you should write about in your document.
- Jot down a major topic or section topic line, such as "benefits of outlines."
- Below your major topic, place the topic words or phrases in sequence (the order in which you think you will write about them) to produce a rough outline of your document.
- Expand your words and phrase to create full points.
- Add any additional related points and subtopic points. (In most instances, you will find them in your clustering. However, sometimes the act of moving from clustering to outline jogs your memory and helps you discover other points.)
- Review your draft outline and revise it as required based on your purpose, audience, and project scope; delete any irrelevant points; and fill in any other gaps between outline points with topics that come to mind as you review your outline.

Once you have completed your outline, continue to read.

If you are so inclined, you can try to write based on your outline. Treat each outline point and subpoint as the opening line of a directed freefall, and write from point to point. You don't have to write as quickly or subconsciously as you do when you freefall, but try to resist the urge to revise as you write. In other words, keep your writer separate from your editor.

If you are in the mood to read, however, carry on. As promised, we will look at shortcuts that will help you prepare, research, and outline short documents such as e-mail messages and memos.

Chapter 7: Writing E-mail Messages

This book will cover writing sentences; constructing paragraphs; using active and passive voice; writing in a concise, focused manner; starting with purpose; conveying a clear call to action; and other topics. You might want to read all of that before you read about writing e-mail messages. However, from writing workshops I've conducted, I know those who primarily write short messages sometimes feel that following the writing process will add significantly to the time they spend writing e-mail messages. So I want to show you the W5 e-mail writing shortcut.

You will still follow the writing process—that's crucial to becoming an effective writer. By answering the W5 questions—who, what, where, when, and why—you will, however, shortcut the full process.

W5 preparation, research, and organization

When writing short documents—such as e-mail messages—and when you do not have to do any, or much, external research, you can reduce the first three steps of the writing process—preparation, research, and organization—to a few minutes using the W5 shortcut method. You then write your message, edit it as may be required, and click send.

W5 stands for who, what, where, when, and why (and sometimes how) and is the foundation of journalism. Answers to the W5 questions are used to outline the lead or opening of any news article. Journalists, in fact, will tell you they do not start writing any article until they have answers to the W5 in place.

There are times journalists find multiple W5 elements (I'll include multiple W5 questions in the e-mail writing exercises), or need more than the basic W5 points, before they can write stories. There are times when they do not use all the W5 points they find. Either way, W5 is the place to start—and I am suggesting that W5 should be the foundation of all business writing too, especially short e-mail messages.

W5 news article outline

So let's see W5 in action. Take a moment to review the following W5 news article outline:

- **Who**? Russians
- **What**? Held impromptu memorial services; killed 39 people and stirred fears of a revival of terrorism here
- **Where**? At two subway stations in Moscow
- **When**? On Tuesday; brazen attacks a day earlier
- **Why**? Suicide bombers conducted brazen attacks

From this W5 comes the article lead in *The New York Times*, March 30, 2010:

> Russians held impromptu memorial services on Tuesday at two subway stations in Moscow where suicide bombers conducted brazen attacks a day earlier that killed 39 people and stirred fears of a revival of terrorism here.

Of course, the full article expands on the W5 and quotes various sources; however, once you have the W5, you have the foundation of the story. And sometimes, once you have the W5, you have the entire story. So the W5 can be the foundation of anything you write and, at times, your W5 can be all you need to write about.

Applying W5 to e-mail

Before you write anything, I suggest you answer the W5 questions, even if you go through the entire writing process first. Answering the W5 questions can help you focus on your purpose, audience, and topic, as well as what you need by way of feedback, action, or reply.

When it comes to writing e-mail, answering the W5 questions can often replace much of the writing process. Answering the W5 questions allows you to think about these points:

- Your audience (*who*)
- Your purpose (*why*)
- Your topic or subject (*what*)

- *When, where* (and perhaps *how*) any action, feedback, or reply should take place

Although it's called the W5, I suggest you toss the sixth W into the mix—how. Answering how helps you determine if you need to give the reader explicit instructions concerning any action you require. In short, answering W5 questions lets you prepare, conduct internal research, and organize your thoughts before you write. Once you've answered the W5 questions, you can take these steps:

- Review your answers and decide what you will include and what you will exclude when writing your message
- Arrange your points in the order in which you should address them—your formal outline
- Write from point to point
- Revise as may be required
- Hit send

You can use the W5 for writing any short message: a thank you note, an apology, a complaint, or an information request. You can also set up a meeting, invite someone to an event, request a project status update, and so on. You can even use W5 to help write sales and marketing messages, although you will most likely have to cover additional points in your sales and marketing material.

What are readers looking for?

When writing, you try to achieve your purpose. At the same time, you should think about what your readers are looking for and expect. What your readers would be looking for is probably the same thing you would be looking for when you receive an e-mail message. Readers would be looking for the following elements:

- A subject line that captures their attention
- Your purpose, clearly stated in the opening paragraph: what the message is about and why it is being written
- A well-organized, clear, concise, focused piece of writing that maintains interest

- A message length that is appropriate for the topic and purpose of the message; short messages are approximately three to five paragraphs in length
- A closing paragraph that lets readers know if any action is required; if so, who takes it, by when, where, and possibly how
- Proper tone in relation to the message and your audience

All of this comes from preparation, research, and organization. Or in the case of e-mail, from answering your W5 questions before you write. With that in mind, let's go through the W5 process for several e-mail messages and do some writing. There are some sample e-mail messages at the end of this chapter; however, try the exercises below before you read the sample messages.

The thank you note

I'd like you to think of someone to whom you owe a thank you note or whom you would like to thank for a personal or business kindness. Before you do the exercise, make sure you have the name of the person in mind and that you know what that person did to earn your thanks.

Once you are ready, write point form answers to the questions below (I've included multiple W5 questions) on a sheet of paper or in a word processing file.

- Whom do you want to thank? (Name the person, and note that person's relationship to you.)
- What did that person do; what action did that person take?
- Where did it take place?
- When did it take place?
- What benefit did you derive from the action?
- What was your primary feeling or emotion?
- Why do you want to thank him or her?
- What overt action, if any, do you want the recipient to take upon reading your e-mail? When and where should it take place?
- Should (how should) the recipient let you know she is taking it?
- What covert action (also known as your hidden agenda), if any, do you want to take place?

Once you have answered the W5 questions, continue to read.

Before we move on, let's examine that last question. Remember all those thank you notes that you sent to your grandparents when you were a child? You sent them after receiving birthday or other holiday-related or special-occasion gifts from them. Although you were truly grateful (or so your parents told you), you probably resisted writing the note—until your parents told you that you might not receive more gifts unless you sent a thank you note. So your hidden agenda was to receive more gifts. But you didn't say that in your thank you note, did you?

It happens in business too.

Before you write anything, you should know what action you want to take place, if anything, and if there are any deeper reasons for writing. You do not necessarily have to address those deeper reasons, but you should be aware of them; that awareness will help you strike the right tone in your message. (More about tone later in the book.)

You probably think you can write a simple thank you note without answering the W5 questions first. You most likely can. What I want you to know is that your brain is going to try to answer them anyway, with or without your active participation. It is ineffective, however, to have your brain thinking about answers to those questions as you are writing.

Just as you need to separate the writer from the editor, you want to separate the planner/researcher from the writer. Obviously, the more complex the message you are writing, the more important it is that you do so. I am asking you to start the separation process here, with a simple message, so you can learn how to do it. Then do it whenever you write, so you can develop the separation habit.

What you did when answering the W5

When you answered the above W5 questions, you started to go through the writing process. Specifically, here is what you did:

- Prepared by establishing your primary purpose: why you were writing, what actions, if any, you wanted to see occur
- Assessed your audience: who they were, what they did, where and when it happened

- Determined the detail to be included in the note: how you felt, what benefit you derived, what action you wanted the reader to take
- Conducted internal research using your memory as the source of information

After jotting down point form notes in answer to the questions, you are almost organized. You probably have more information than you want to use in your final e-mail message, but part of getting organized is deciding what information you want to include and want to exclude. In fact, many writers will tell you that having more information than you need to use is a good place to be because it lets you think about what you need to say and don't need to say, which helps you focus.

If you are working on paper, highlight the points that you want to address in your thank you note. Once you have completed your highlighting, transfer your points to a word processing document. If you are working on your computer, save your research and create a new file. Copy and paste your research into the new file and delete any points you don't have to express. (Save your original research in case you delete material that you later decide you need. This way, you will have it handy rather than having to recreate it.)

Decide if you are going to start writing by recreating the event, by describing your feelings, or by detailing the benefits you have derived. It's your choice. The one thing you want to do, though, is get to your purpose—"thank you"—in the first paragraph. After all, your purpose is to thank your reader, so don't wait until the end of your message to achieve your purpose.

Then arrange your points in the order in which you will address them. With that, you have prepared an outline so that your writing will unfold in a focused, logical manner.

Write and then revise

Since this is a short thank you note, you do not have to consider layout or design. You can simply write from outline point to outline point, expanding each point into sentences and paragraphs. Write with spell check and grammar check turned off. So when you are ready, write your thank you note.

Once you have written your thank you note, continue to read.

Once you have completed the first draft of your thank you note, review your paragraphing. Ensure that each paragraph contains no more than one significant point, or ensure that the points contained in each paragraph are directly related. (See Chapter 9: Paragraphs and Transitions.)

Revise with your reader and topic in mind. Ensure that the tone is appropriate to the subject and that your document is clear, concise, and focused, and supports your purpose. Check spelling and grammar.

Finally, if this is an e-mail, add a subject line. Think of your subject line as an attention-grabbing headline. But remember, the subject line does not have to be in-your-face to grab attention. It should be tone appropriate, address your purpose, and pique the curiosity of the recipient. And you are done

It is possible, even probable, that the entire process took longer than it would have taken you to just sit down and write the thank you note off the top of your head. I hope, though, that the note you have written is as effective, if not more effective, than the note you would have written had you just started with the blank screen. In addition, the more you practice this process, the less time it will take to prepare, research, and outline your short messages.

The more prepared you are, the more complete your research is, and the more detailed your outline is, the less time you will spend writing. That makes you more efficient.

The more prepared you are, the more complete your research is, the more detailed the outline is, the clearer, more concise, and focused your writing will be. That makes you more effective.

The clearer, more concise, and focused your writing is, the less time you will spend revising—and the time you do spend revising will be more productive. But none of this will happen magically. It will only happen if you practice the full or short-cut five-step writing process repeatedly.

Sample thank you note

Before we move on, let's look at a thank you note:

Subject: Thank you for the opportunity

I wish to thank you for the confidence you have shown in me by promoting me to dispatch. I am excited about the challenges this position offers and look forward to learning as fast as I can so that I can contribute to the success of the company.

Your confidence in me is appreciated. I will work hard to meet your expectations, as this is a great opportunity.

Sincerely,
Janice Lake

Notice how the subject line conveys a clear sense of purpose. It does not just say "thank you" but it includes "the opportunity." The why, or the reason the writer is writing, is there—*thank you*—as is what the writer is thanking the reader for—*the opportunity*. When you write, look at your W5 and try to convey the most important elements in your subject line.

Just as the body of a report elaborates on a report's executive summary, as you will see, the opening paragraph of an e-mail message elaborates on the most important elements of the subject line. In this case we see more of the why and what in the opening line. Notice how the rest of the opening paragraph supports that opening line. This is called focus. In other words, the message does not digress into other topics. And notice how the closing paragraph acts as a summary of the message, just as (as you will see) a conclusion summarizes a report.

This repetition, restatement, and elaboration, without becoming redundant, is required to achieve focus and to ensure the reader gets your message. You will see this method used in effective e-mail messages, letters, proposals, and reports.

In this particular message, there is no call to action and no request for feedback, nor does the message require one.

If you are saying you could have written the thank you note without asking the W5 questions, I will not argue with you. Without asking the W5 questions, you would have written a different message—similar, perhaps, but different. Also, the more complex a message is, the more important it is to ask the W5 questions before you write. In short, develop a W5 habit no matter what you want to write and you will be more likely to ask, and answer, the questions before you write important business e-mail messages.

With that in mind, let's try two more messages—an apology note and a complaint.

The apology note

Think of someone to whom you owe an apology—business or personal—and write that person an e-mail message. Before you begin, answer the following W5 questions (and any others you may feel are appropriate):

- To whom are you writing? (What is your relationship to that person?)
- What did you do that you need to apologize for?
- Where did it take place?
- When did it take place?
- Why are you writing?
- Why do you want to apologize?
- What is your primary feeling or emotion?
- What is the recipient's primary feeling or emotion?
- What action, if any, do you want to take place next, or hope will take place next?
- Where and when should it take place?
- What, if any, is your hidden agenda?

Follow the process outlined in the thank you note exercise and write your e-mail. Don't forget to include a subject line.

> **Once you have written your apology note, continue to read.**

Before you revise your document, review your "why." This is your purpose. Make sure you are alluding to your "why" in your subject line and opening paragraph. In fact, make sure you get your purpose into any document you are writing as early on as possible.

The complaint e-mail

Let's complain or ask that a situation be rectified. You choose the topic:

- Did you have problems obtaining this book?

- Are you currently dealing with a problem with a superior or subordinate?
- Are you having any work-related problems that are irking you?
- Have you recently had problems at a retail outlet or with a product or service?
- Are you having problems with City Hall or any other level of government?
- Are you having problems with a spouse, partner, or child?
- Is there any other problem you would like to complain about or have rectified?

Sometimes, when you want to complain or want a situation to be rectified, especially if you've been battling for ages, you have to write a longer message. But in this particular exercise, we are going to be short, succinct, and reasonable.

With that in mind, focus on the complaint or situation you want rectified and answer the following questions:

- To whom are you writing? (What is your relationship?)
- Why are you writing?
- What are you complaining about?
- Where did this take place?
- When did this take place?
- Why did this take place?
- What is your primary feeling or emotion?
- What do you want to have rectified?
- Why do you want a resolution?
- What action would it take to satisfy you?
- When should this be done by? Where should it be done?
- What action will you take if this is not rectified?
- Did you previously complain to this person about this situation? If so, where and when? With what result?

Follow the thank you note process and write. Don't forget to delete any points you don't need to include in your message. Also, ensure your purpose is clear and up front in your subject line and opening sentence or paragraph.

> **Once you have written your complaint note, continue to read.**

Final e-mail exercise

Before you look at the sample e-mail messages at the end of this chapter, take some time and complete one more e-mail writing exercise. For this final exercise, I'd like you to write a business or work-related e-mail message. Feel free to come up with your own idea for this e-mail message, but if you need an idea, here are some suggestions you can choose from:

- Arrange a meeting
- Solicit a quote
- Query a tardy supplier
- Request an overdue payment
- Report on progress to a colleague, supplier, vendor
- Move back a project deadline
- Request assistance on a project

Before you write, come up with the W5 questions you want to answer to help you think about your reader, conduct internal research, and organize your thoughts. Doing these tasks first will help you focus your writing, so you should spend less time revising. You will still revise, but you will be starting with a solid first draft. If you feel you need a bit of help writing sentences, take a sneak peek at Chapter 8 (Constructing Sentences).

> **Once you have written your work-related note, continue to read.**

Sample e-mail messages

On the next few pages are several sample e-mail messages. Deconstruct them to see if you can find the who, what, where, when, why, and/or how. Not all elements will be found in every message. Part of your job, as mentioned, is to determine what to put in and what to leave out of anything you write. Also, ask yourself

- if the "why" or purpose of the e-mail message is clear and up front,
- if benefits and/or consequences (or anything else that might influence attitude) are detailed,
- if the action—if action is required—is clear.

Note: Avoid anger, sarcasm, tongue-in-cheek remarks, or extreme emotion in business writing. However, when writing a consumer-to-business (or consumer-to-politician) message, you might get away with a modest amount of emotion or gentle humor. For instance, I like the humorous subject line of the e-mail below, but notice how it is related to the subject matter and how the message starts with a clear purpose.

E-mail message samples

> **Subject**: Take this snow and shovel it!
>
> Dear Municipal Councilor Johnson,
>
> I'm writing to resolve the issue about snow removal after a snowfall.
>
> During the recent heavy snowfall, a few of my neighbors shoveled snow from their driveways and dumped it on city property. Unfortunately, they piled their snow at the front and back of other people's vehicles, making it difficult to exit the parking spaces. This became a point of frustration for many of the car owners.
>
> Would your office be able to send out notices to the residents of my neighborhood to remind them that there is a snow removal bylaw they must adhere to? If you could provide me with a response by the end of the week, it would be greatly appreciated.
>
> Sincerely,
> Sidney Smith

◘ ◘ ◘

Subject: Sorry for missing lunch

Dear Janine,

After speaking to your husband, I realize that my absence from a recent networking lunch that we had agreed to attend upset you and I would like to apologize for missing the gathering.

There were several last minute scheduling changes at work, but I should have called you. I am sorry for not doing so.

Your friendship means a great deal to me. I look forward to seeing you at lunch next month.

Sincerely,
Terri

◩   ◩   ◩

Subject: Sincerest appreciation for your help

Dear Laura,

It has been a week since I started my new job and I could not have landed the promotion without your help. I just wanted to thank you for your support. Because of your assistance, I was able to produce significant results and impress our supervisor who gave me the recommendation that opened the door to the job interview.

I would like to invite you for dinner this weekend and thank you personally. Please let me know over the next day or two if you are available. You can e-mail or call me.

Best regards,
Sally

◩   ◩   ◩

Subject: Apology for missing the lab meeting

Dear Dr. Jones,

I apologize for missing the lab meeting this morning and for the inconvenience I may have caused. Unfortunately, the subway I was on got stuck at Bloor and Yonge and was out of service for 40 minutes.

I was supposed to share the results of my work with my colleagues. I will e-mail my results later today to you and to my lab partners so that they have the most up-to-date information on my project.

If you have any questions about my results, please e-mail me or talk to me at the next lab meeting.

Sincerely,
Sally

◙   ◙   ◙

Subject: Written Warning

It has become necessary to again remind you of your responsibilities. Since issuing a verbal warning two weeks ago, we have not seen improvements in the following areas:

- Arriving at work at the scheduled time
- Matching your paperwork to the product being loaded
- Giving appropriate notice of non-work-related appointments

Immediate improvements in these areas are expected. They are necessary to ensure customer satisfaction. Your work-related performance will be reviewed daily.

Failure to comply with this request immediately will lead to further disciplinary action up to, and including, termination. If you have any questions, email me.

Sincerely,
Jane Lake

◙   ◙   ◙

Subject: Overdue payment reminder

Dear Ms. Lam,

Our records indicate that payment of your account in the amount of $6,890 is 30 days overdue. A copy of invoice #181 is attached.

If the payment has been forwarded, please disregard this e-mail. Otherwise, please submit payment by October 23.

If you are unable to submit your payment, please e-mail or call (416) 555-1212 so that we can discuss and resolve the issue. Thank you for your cooperation.

Sincerely,
Sally Arnold

◙   ◙   ◙

Subject: Tiffany sofa payment

Dear Ms. Williams,

Furniture Gallery is confident that you are enjoying the Tiffany sofa that you purchased last March at the Main Street location. You took advantage of our "no money down for six months" special and we are now at the end of the sixth month. So you can continue to enjoy the sofa, we need to receive your first payment by March 14.

You can make your payment by cash, check, or credit card (Visa or MasterCard) at the Main Street location. If you have any questions, please reply to this e-mail or call (416) 555-1212.

Sincerely,
Gail Jones

◙   ◙   ◙

The apology e-mail below is particularly effective. The writer explains what happened, takes full responsibility and offers the reader appropriate compensation. He also assures the reader it will not happen again—all in three focused, concise paragraphs.

Subject: Apologies for missing Saturday's lesson

Dear Mr. Tanaka,

I would like to apologize for my scheduling mistake. During our last meeting, we decided to conduct our next training session on Saturday. I did not have my day planner with me so I could not record the date. Because we usually meet Sundays, the date slipped my mind. This does not excuse what happened and I assure you that it will not happen again.

Your time is valuable, so to compensate you for the lost time and the inconvenience there will be no charge for the next lesson.

I apologize again for my scheduling mistake and look forward to seeing you on Sunday, March 14, at 1 pm.

Regards,
George Thompson

Chapter 8: Constructing Sentences

In the beginning was the word. It was quickly followed by the sentence. Which, of course, was followed by the paragraph.

Do you know what the shortest sentence in the Bible is? Two words: *Jesus wept.* The sentence has a subject (*Jesus*) and a verb (*wept*). In theory, that is all a sentence needs to be complete.

Where, however, is the subject in the following two-word sentence?

Do it!

The subject, *you*, in a command or imperative is understood. Everyone who hears the simple command *Do it!* understands it to mean *You do it.* Drop the *you*, start the sentence with the verb (to do), and the sentence packs a more powerful punch.

Without a subject (real or implied) and verb, you have a sentence fragment:

Because I.
Over there.
The officer.

However, look at the third sentence in this chapter:

Which, of course, was followed by the paragraph.

When you read it, did you notice that it was a sentence fragment? (Where is the subject?) Did it feel like a fragment when you read it? Even if it did, was it effective? Does it feel like a fragment now that you are reading it out of context?

Although sentence fragments can be used effectively, particularly in fiction and advertising, seldom will you use them in business writing. If they are not used appropriately—for a conscious effect or to emphasize a particular point—they can create disjointed writing and can cause miscommunication and confusion.

Part of your goal as a business writer is to become aware of, and correct, sentence faults and other problems that can interfere with clear, concise communication. You do this when editing your work. In other words, don't get hung up on fixing them as you write. That will thwart your writing efficiency. At the same time, if you follow the writing process, especially the creation of detailed outlines, you will bring greater clarity to your writing— and so have fewer revisions to make when editing.

While grammar and spelling count, this is not a book about grammar and spelling. This is a business writing and writing-process book. With that in mind, I will not spend much time on particular sentence faults. We will, however, look at the active and passive voice and, later in the book, at ways to make your writing as concise as possible. In addition, there are examples of how to construct effective sentences in this chapter.

Active versus passive voice

Read the two passages below. What is different about them? What is similar?

> The Highway Department is building a new bridge in River Hollow. The backhoe digs deep holes. The cement mixer pours in concrete to make the supports.
>
> Carefully Carlton picks up steel girders with his crane and lays them across the supports.
>
> Bulldozers push up the surrounding ground to make a road. The grading machine smoothes the slope, and the asphalt spreader pours down a layer of blacktop. Brian's steamroller comes last to smooth it flat and even. Dennis and Darlene haul away the extra dirt in their dump truck.

◾ ◾ ◾

> Research into new advertising promotions that could boost company sales was initiated by marketing last spring.
>
> A list of primary media read by our Target Market was compiled by Susan McMillan. Creative ideas were

produced by the copywriting department. A campaign was designed by Frank Myers, the art director, and was launched in the summer.

Encouraging have been the sales results to date.

Does the first passage remind you of a grade one reader? If you are old enough to have gone on adventures with Dick and Jane, it might remind you of those famous sentences that you read when you were first learning to read:

See Dick. See Jane. See Dick run. See Jane run. See Spot. See Spot run. Hear Spot bark.

The sentences above are clear and concise. But are they effective? Or are they boring and monotonous? Could you imagine reading an entire report with sentences written only like the ones in the first or the second passage above?

In the first passage, the simple sentences are written in the active voice, which can be used to create short, direct sentences. The second passage is written entirely in the passive voice, which makes for longer, more awkward sentences that distance the reader from who did what.

While the most effective sentences are generally written in the active voice, effective writing requires variety—a mix of active and passive voice, a mix of complex and simple sentences, and the use of sentences of various lengths.

Active voice

We are not going to get bogged down in grammatical terms; however, I need to use two: *subject* and *verb*. In the active voice, the *subject* performs the action expressed in the **verb**. In other words, the subject acts, as in the examples below:

The dog **bit** the boy.

Terri **will present** her research at the conference.

We **received** your shipment two days late, which caused delays.

You **sent** the shipment two days late, which caused delays.

Scientists **have conducted** experiments to test the hypothesis.

Passive voice

In sentences written in the passive voice, the *subject* receives the action expressed by the **verb**. The agent performing the action may appear in a "by the..." phrase or may be omitted entirely.

The boy **was bitten** by the dog.

Research **will be presented** by Terri at the conference.

Your payment **was received** two days late, which caused delays.

Experiments **have been conducted** to test the hypothesis.

Notice the agents committing the action are missing from the last two sentenced. Here are the last two sentences with the "by the" agents included:

Your payment was received two days late by the accounting department, which caused delays.

Experiments have been conducted by the scientists to test the hypothesis.

Do you need "by the accounting department" or "by the scientists" in the above sentences? The sentences are grammatically correct even without the agents. If, however, it was important for the reader to know that the accounting department did not receive the payments, or that scientists conducted the experiments, then the agents should be included. If not, no problem leaving the agents out.

Leaving the scientists out of the second sentence puts the focus on the experiments and why they were conducted. There is nothing wrong with this focus, if that is where you want to put it. In other words, where you put your emphasis or focus, and the voice you use, should be conscious decisions.

Having said that, you should know that the passive voice can create awkward sentences and cause readers to become confused. Sentences written in the active voice require fewer words than those written in the passive voice. This makes for writing that is more concise. In addition, sentences in the active voice are generally clearer and more direct than those in the passive voice.

The passive voice can allow writers to compose without using personal pronouns or names of people or groups (as with the scientists and accounting department sentences).This can help create the appearance of an objective, fact-based discourse. But the passive voice can also be used to deflect blame or avoid responsibility, which is not always warranted, as in the following sentence:

> Seeking to lay off workers without taking the blame,
> consultants were hired to break the bad news.

Who was seeking to lay off workers? The consultants? That's what it looks like in this sentence. However, the CEO was more likely responsible. If that is the case, leaving out the agent creates a misleading sentence that avoids allocating proper responsibility. So let's use active voice and include the responsible party:

> Seeking to lay off workers without taking the blame, the
> CEO hired consultants to break the bad news.

Being direct can be an important aspect of business discourse. On the other hand, there are times when being indirect is preferable. If there is no clear agent, then there is no clear blame, and sometimes it is necessary to point out a problem without pointing fingers, as in these examples:

> Several mistakes were made before the trains collided.

> The quota was not met last month, so monthly bonuses
> have been withheld.

In the train example: Imagine that a train collision is under review. It is obvious that the trains should not have collided. The spokesperson for the railway company cannot deny that a collision has occurred. However, the spokesperson cannot say who made mistakes that caused the collision until the accident review is completed. Instead, she resorts to the passive voice and leaves out the agent so she does not allocate blame. If she had included the agent, she might have said something like this:

> Several mistakes were made by the eastbound engineer
> before the trains collided.

And if she had used the active voice, she might have said this:

> The eastbound engineer made several mistakes before
> the trains collided.

In the quota example: The person making the announcement might know which person or department did not meet quota, but has chosen not to say it publicly. Also, notice that the person making the announcement has not credited an individual—the CEO or a specific manager—for withholding bonuses. What we have here is the withholding of two agents and the double use of passive voice in one sentence, but it is not necessarily doublespeak. You might call it politically sensitive communication.

Choosing the passive voice

As mentioned, the passive voice highlights what is acted upon rather than focusing on the agent performing the action. It makes sense when the agent performing the action is obvious, unknown, or unimportant. It also makes sense when a writer wishes to postpone mentioning the agent until the last part of the sentence, or to avoid mentioning the agent at all.

In the examples below, the passive voice makes sense if the agent is less important than the action and what is acted upon.

> **Active**: The dispatcher notified police only minutes after
> three prisoners had escaped.

Passive: Police were notified only minutes after three prisoners had escaped.

If it is more important to know how long it took for the police to be notified than it is to know who notified the police, the passive voice makes sense. If there was some question as to who notified the police, and if that was more important than how long it took for the police to be notified, the active voice would make sense.

In the next sentence, what is more important: the spruce budworm or the irrevocable damage?

Active: The spruce budworm has irrevocably damaged vast expanses of Cape Breton forests.

Passive: Vast expanses of Cape Breton forests have been irrevocably damaged by the spruce budworm.

In the passive voice sentence, the emphasis is on the damage to the forests, not the cause of the damage. If, however, you wanted to warn people about the spruce budworm, the active voice would make more sense.

When choosing between the active and passive voice, what you want to do is keep the reader, your topic, and your purpose in mind. Also, think about clarity and conciseness. In other words, make conscious decisions concerning the use of the active and passive voice. But beware of using the passive voice to mask issues that should be addressed and don't overuse the passive voice.

Convert passive to active

Take a moment and convert the passive voice sentences below to active voice. If you are not sure that you have done it correctly, set grammar checker to flag passive constructions and grammar check your revised sentences. You can also look at the revised sentences at the end of this chapter.

The entrance exam was failed by more than one third of the applicants to the school.

The brakes were slammed on by her as the car sped downhill.

Your bicycle has been damaged.

(The agent has been omitted. Who did the damage? Edit the sentence as if you did and edit it as if a thief has damaged the bicycle.)

Action on the bill is being considered by the committee.

By then, the soundtrack will have been completely remixed by the sound engineers.

To satisfy the instructor's demands for legibility, the paper was written on a computer.

(Before revising this, ask who was satisfying the instructor? The paper? Or the person writing the paper? Then edit the sentence.)

Once you have converted the passive sentences to active voice, continue to read.

How to construct a sentence

As I mentioned, this is not a grammar book. I want to take a moment, however, to review the foundation of the sentence. At minimum, the sentence requires a subject and a verb (action). In *I laughed,* *I* is the subject; *laughed* is the verb. But two-word sentences generally don't cut it in business writing. So let's review a sentence that includes a *subject*, a **verb**, and a third component—the <u>object</u>.

The boy **kicked** <u>the soccer ball</u>.

The boy is our subject (the person who does the action). **Kicked** is the verb or action. <u>The soccer ball</u> is our object, that which receives the action. I call these three elements "the heart of the sentence." If you ever feel that your sentences are getting too complex, find the heart. Once you have the heart, you can expand your sentence logically and keep the meaning clear. For instance, where did the ball go when the boy kicked it?

The boy kicked the soccer ball through the window.

What happened to the window?

> The boy kicked the soccer ball through the window,
> which shattered into a thousand pieces.

Tell me more about this boy:

> The tall, thin, Caucasian boy kicked the soccer ball
> through the window, which shattered into a thousand
> pieces.

Do you see how our sentence is becoming more complex? It is easy to understand, however, because we can still identify the heart of the sentence. Now imagine that this action was committed by a criminal.

> The tall, thin, armed and dangerous Caucasian boy
> kicked the soccer ball through the window, which
> shattered into a thousand pieces.

What happened next?

> The tall, thin, armed and dangerous Caucasian boy
> kicked the soccer ball through the window, which
> shattered into a thousand pieces, and then he fled the
> scene.

Notice we now have two "hearts" combined. Let me simplify them for you:

> The boy kicked the soccer ball through the window.

> He fled the scene.

Two subjects, two verbs, two objects. One sentence. Meaning is still clear because we let one heart beat, so to speak, and then the other. So if you think sentences are running away on you, identify your subject and verb and build from there. If you have more than one subject and verb, identify each of them and determine how best to let them beat. Joined or as two separate sentences. If the complex sentence feels like it is unclear, separate the two hearts:

> The tall, thin, armed and dangerous Caucasian boy kicked the soccer ball through the window, which shattered into a thousand pieces. Then he fled the scene.

Keep this in mind as you try the other writing exercises in this book and as you write and edit your work.

Passive voice converted to active voice

The passive sentences presented earlier in this chapter have been converted to the active voice.

> More than one third of the applicants to the school failed the entrance exam.

> She slammed on the brakes as the car sped downhill.

> I have damaged your bicycle.
> The thief damaged your bicycle.

> The committee is considering action on the bill.

> By then, the sound engineers will have completely remixed the soundtrack.

> I wrote the paper on a computer to satisfy the instructor's demands for legibility.

> The student wrote the paper on a computer to satisfy the instructor's demands for legibility.

Chapter 9: Paragraphs and Transitions

A paragraph is a collection of sentences organized around a clearly defined topic. If you are writing a long document, each paragraph topic will be a subtopic of, or somehow related to, the subject of the document you are writing.

The paragraph performs three functions:
1. Develops the unit of thought stated in the topic sentence
2. Provides a logical break in the material
3. Creates a visual break on the page, thus signaling a new topic

Generally, the paragraph starts with a topic sentence. Often, this topic sentence is an important outline point converted into a complete sentence. The topic sentence states the paragraph's main idea. The rest of the paragraph supports and develops the idea.

The topic sentence is often the first sentence in a paragraph because it tells the reader what the paragraph is about. However, the topic sentence can be used to end a paragraph—almost like a punch line. Occasionally, the topic sentence can be found in the middle of the paragraph. There would be some build up to the topic sentence, the topic sentence, and then some support of the topic.

Topic at the beginning

Here is an example of writing with the topic sentence at the beginning of each paragraph:

> *The cost of orientation, health and safety, and customer service training for new Customer Service Representatives (CSRs) is significant.* The organization must cover the price of classroom facilities, instructors, and manuals and must pay employees their full salary, while they are non-productive, during the three-week training period.

> *If the company is to break even on its investment in training*, employees must stay in the job for which they have been hired for at least one year, according to our analysis (see attached PDF). However, on average, customer service representatives leave the company within nine months of hiring. Not only is the company losing money on employee training, we are also paying exorbitant recruitment costs to fill each vacancy.
>
> *To increase the return on investment (ROI) for training new CSRs*, the committee proposes that the following three recommendations be implemented within three months:
> 1. Recommendation one....
> 2. Recommendation two....
> 3. Recommendation three....

Notice how the first sentence of the first paragraph establishes both the subject of the document as well as the topic of the paragraph: "The cost of... is significant." I suspect you could imagine this sentence being used to establish the topic about almost any paragraph dealing with cost issues, such as: *The cost of purchasing parts from our current supplier is significant.* In short, the sentence raises an issue, which creates expectations that the document will explain why the cost of whatever is significant and will most likely suggest how the issue can be resolved. The rest of the paragraph explains why the cost is significant and the document goes on to suggests how to solve the problem.

The opening sentence of the second paragraph does something interesting. It tells us the circumstances that must occur if we are to solve the problem and offers us proof. It does not, however, cram the proof into the document: "If the company is to break even on its investment in training, employees must stay in the job for which they have been hired for at least one year, according to our analysis (see attached PDF)."

It often makes sense to attach complex details to an e-mail message or to include them in an appendix in a report. If readers believe you are addressing a valid issue, they will have no need to get bogged down in the details that prove it. By attaching the PDF, the writer can move quickly from the problem to the solution while offering skeptics proof in the attached document or report appendix.

Finally, notice how the third paragraph consists of a topic sentence and three points. (There will be more on when and why to use bullet points or numbered points later in this chapter.)

Topic at the end

Here is an example of writing with the topic sentence at the end of the paragraph:

> Energy does more than simply make our lives more comfortable and convenient. If you wanted to reverse or stop economic progress, the surest way to do so would be to cut off the nation's oil resources. The country would plummet into the abyss of economic ruin. *In short, our economy is energy-based.*

Often—not always—opening paragraphs in e-mail messages, letters, executive summaries of reports, and other documents place the topic sentence at the end of the paragraph. This lets the writer set the stage with a few lines that build up to the topic and purpose of the document.

Your topic and purpose can be made clear in the first line of the first paragraph, the last line of the first paragraph, or even part way through your first paragraph. The important thing is that, almost without exception, the reader needs to know what you are writing about (your topic) and why (your purpose) by the end of the opening paragraph. (There will be more on purpose later in the book.)

Paragraph length

The length of each paragraph should aid the reader's understanding of the idea addressed. A series of very short paragraphs can indicate poor organization and underdeveloped thoughts. Too many long paragraphs, however, can fail to provide the reader with manageable subdivisions of thought. The occasional one-sentence paragraph is acceptable if it is used for effect or as a transition between paragraphs. One-sentence paragraphs are also acceptable in short letters and memos—particularly as openings or closings.

With that in mind, read the 220-word paragraph on the next page. It is the executive summary from a report written by a financial analyst for a major bank.

To help you into it, here is the title of the report:

Focus on Health Care: Are Canadians Missing an Opportunity?

Take a moment and think about the expectations that this title raises. Based on this title, what do you expect the report to focus on? (Remember, it was written by a financial analyst, so that should also influence your expectations.) Who is the audience for this report? Why do you think that? Once you've mulled over the above questions, read the executive summary:

ABC Research Co. appears to have put a greater emphasis on products that cater to the heath-care industry. ABC estimates that the U.S. market for furniture in the health-care industry to be approximately $1.7 billion and that the majority of this market is supplied by a fragmented regional supply base. The market is roughly split 50/50 between traditional office furniture and clinical furniture. ABC indicated that the market is expected to probably grow by 50% over the next seven years, driven by needs of an aging population and needed replacement of obsolete aging facilities, many of which are now 20 to 30 years old. Expectations of ABC are that there will be a greater growth within the clinical segment of the furniture market. Although the Canadian manufacturers have talked about focusing on other end markets in the U.S. including government, education, and health care, it appears that the U.S. manufacturers have made more significant investments at least in targeting the health-care market specifically, given the clinical products they are offering to complement their traditional office furniture products. Given the expected growth in the health-care market, we wonder whether the Canadian manufacturers should perhaps consider acquiring small U.S. suppliers with heavy health care exposure as a way to increase penetration into this segment of the market.

Expectations met or dashed?

Were your expectations, based on the title, met or dashed? Did the paragraph start with (or end with) a topic sentence? Did the writing support (or build up to) the topic?

At what point in the executive summary did it occur to you that this report was about the health-care *furniture* industry? At what point did it occur to you that the issue is whether Canadian furniture manufacturers (not Canadians generally) were missing the opportunity to move into the American health-care furniture market?

What did you make of all those wiggle words—"appears," "probably," "wonder," "should," "perhaps," and so on. Do they create confidence in the content and conclusions expressed? And what of the conclusion or recommendation? Is it as powerful as it could be?

What is the purpose of the report? Is it achieved? Does the writing capture the attention of readers, hold their interest, or influence their attitudes? If so, does it do it well? Does it clearly let them know what action they should take based on the arguments presented?

Let's review the three functions of the paragraph:

1. Develops the unit of thought stated in the topic sentence
2. Provides a logical break in the material
3. Creates a visual break on the page, thus signaling a new topic.

Now turn back to the ABC executive summary. What is the topic? Can you even find a topic sentence? Or are there several topics at work here? If so, is there a logical break in the material between topics? What is your opinion of the visual breaks, or should I say the lack thereof?

When presented with this wall of words, how did you, as the reader, feel? I admit that reading this paragraph is not as intimidating as reading Joseph Conrad (many of his paragraphs run on for pages), but my eyes scream for some visual relief every time I see this paragraph. Oh no, I think, if the entire document is going to look like this, then I don't want to read it.

Although this is not a book about layout and design, you need to know that the look of your document can affect your reader's attitude toward your writing—even before he begins to read (or perhaps not read, if the writing looks like an impenetrable wall of words).

Paragraph exercise

With that in mind, take a shot at editing the executive summary presented above. Your goal is to read the summary, understand it, determine your purpose, organize it (create an outline), and revise it.

If you believe there is more than one topic addressed in the executive summary, turn it into multiple paragraphs. Rewrite sentences. Delete any information that does not advance your purpose. Create clear, concise writing that captures attention, holds interest, influences attitude, and presents a clear call to action based on the facts. Oh, and feel free to give the report a new, more appropriate, title.

There is a sample of a revised executive summary at the end of this chapter. However, tackle this exercise before you read it. Give your internal editor a good workout. And do not be concerned if your take on the revised summary is not the same as the example. No two people would produce the same revised document. The example is simply how one editor would turn the executive summary into a more concise, focused, well-structured document.

> **Once you have revised the executive summary, continue to read.**

Transitions

Transitions help the reader move smoothly from sentence to sentence and paragraph to paragraph. Think of transitions as a two-way indicator, pointing to what has been said and what will be said. In that way, transitions help readers link ideas and clarify the relationship between them. Conversely, a lack of transitions can make for disjointed reading. (*Conversely* is just one of many transitional words and phrases.)

Here are two examples of transitional sentences:

> Having considered the costs and benefits of building a new facility, we move next to the question of adequate staffing.

◼   ◼   ◼

> Even if the new facility can be built at a reasonable cost, there is still the question of adequate staffing.

Transitions do not have to be so overt, nor do they have to be complete sentences. As we shall see, the transitional components of a sentence often appear at the beginning of a sentence; however, they can appear part way through the transitional sentence as well.

Transitions can be achieved by

1. using transitional words or phrases between sentences;
2. using transitional sentences between sentences or, more likely, between paragraphs;
3. repeating keywords or phrases that appear in one sentence in the next sentence;
4. paraphrasing keywords or phrases that appear in one sentence in the next sentence;
5. numbering;
6. summarizing a previous paragraph in a sentence between paragraphs.

Different transitional words or phrases have different functions. For example, *for example* is an excellent transition example. When a sentence begins with "for example," you expect to see the idea that preceded the transition made clear through use of an example or a case in point. In addition, when you see *in addition* at the beginning of a sentence, you expect the writer to add something to the idea or topic. However, when you see the word *however* in a sentence, you expect the information in the "however" sentence to contrast the information that has come before the sentence.

Transition words and phrases are often used at the beginning of sentences. You might, however, also see transition words used part way through a sentence, following the first clause, as *however* is used in this sentence.

The occasional however at the start of sentence is fine. However, if overused at the start of too many sentences in a passage, *however* can feel repetitive. That is one reason you might want to use *however* after the first clause of a sentence.

In fact, the esteemed grammarians Strunk and White in their book, *The Elements of Style*, suggest that one shouldn't start a sentence with however when one means 'nevertheless' or 'on the other hand'. On the other hand, language evolves and modern usage of however when one means 'nevertheless' or 'on the other hand' has become more acceptable.

Transitions in action

With the above information in mind, read the article excerpt on the next page and find the transition words, phrases, sentences, and so on in it.

> Kevin Huber can navigate through his word processing package as fast as almost any other computer user. However, unlike most computer users, Kevin cannot see the keyboard or his monitor. In fact, other than differentiating between intense light and dark shadows, Kevin sees nothing.
>
> Legally blind since birth, Kevin hears what others see thanks to adaptive technologies. Adaptive technologies are tools that translate visual information into audible information for visually challenged computer users.
>
> Kevin has adjusted to his challenge so well that he now works as a client support representative for Microcomputer Science Centre in Mississauga, where he tests new computer technology intended for use by visually challenged persons. He also shows instructors how to train persons with disabilities to compute and surf the Web using adaptive technology.
>
> Like slanted sidewalks, or curb cuts, which are used to make streets more accessible to mobility challenged persons, adaptive technology, or electronic curb cuts, are used to make computers more accessible to physically challenged persons.
>
> Physical challenges can be divided into three categories: visual, hearing, and mobility. Visual challenges range from reduced visual acuity to blindness. Hearing challenges range from slight loss of hearing to deafness. And mobility challenges range from impaired movement of limbs to limited movement of the head and lips.

The transitions are highlighted in a passage at the end of this chapter. However, try to find them before you move to the end of the chapter.

> **Once you have completed the transition exercise, continue to read.**

Now that you are familiar with transitions, review your revised executive summary to see if you can find opportunities for weaving in transitions that will help the reader move more smoothly from point to point. If you can, edit your work again and apply smoother transitions. In addition, run your edited executive summary through your grammar checker. (Make sure your grammar checker is set to stop at passive voice.) If grammar checker stops at a passive sentence, decide if you want to convert it to the active voice. Remember, passive voice is grammatically correct; however, you should consciously choose if you want a sentence to be in the active or the passive voice. In short, make informed, conscious decisions when editing.

Bullet and numbered points

As we saw previously in this chapter, in the topic sentence example about "the cost of orientation, health and safety, and customer service training," there are times when bullet point or numbered point sentences make sense.

Bullet and numbered points are easy to scan and absorb. They make sense when you are making a series of recommendations or when you are giving instructions—especially if the instructions must be performed sequentially. Look at the examples below. They are presented as conventional paragraphs and then as numbered points. Which ones make the most sense to you? Why?

Example I

For you to start juggling, you must do the following: first pick up A in your right hand, then you should pick up B in you left hand, and then you should toss A and then B into the air, catching A as you toss B and catching B and you toss A. Repeat continuously.

For you to start juggling, do the following:
- Pick up A in your right hand
- Pick up B in your left hand
- Toss A into the air
- Toss B into the air while catching A
- Toss A back into the air while catching B
- Repeat continuously

■   ■   ■

Example II

Three habits that improve health are getting eight hours of sleep each night, eating three balanced meals every day, and exercising regularly.

Three habits that improve health are
1. Getting eight hours of sleep each night,
2. Eating three balanced meals every day,
3. Exercising regularly.

The numbered points convey the information in a manner that is easier to scan, absorb, and understand. The shorter lines cause the eye to stop at the end of each point as the brain does a mental check. Then the eye moves to the beginning of the next point and repeats the pattern. With that in mind, look for opportunities to use bullet or numbered points. However, don't overdo it. A page full of bullet points can look almost as tedious to read as the wall-of-words executive summary presented earlier in this chapter. Also:

- Bullet points used for no reason don't make sense.

- If you use them just because you think you should, you could confuse the reader.

- The reader will be looking for a list of instructions or recommendations where no list exists.

- That can be confusing. Enough said, yes?

■   ■   ■

Executive summary: suggested revision

A Focus on the Future of Health-care Furniture: Are Canadian Manufacturers Missing an Opportunity?

Canadian furniture manufacturers want to sell products to the growing U.S. health-care furniture market, but they lag far behind their U.S. counterparts. However, there are ways they can achieve this goal.

Driven by an aging population and the need to replace obsolete facilities, ABC Research Co. estimates that the value of the U.S. market for health-care furniture will grow by 50%, reaching approximately $1.7 billion by 2012. Growth will occur primarily in the clinical segment of this market.

Regional office furniture and clinical furniture manufacturers currently supply the majority of the health-care furniture market, but national American furniture manufacturers have made significant investments in clinical products.

To gain entry into this market, Canadian furniture manufacturers should acquire small U.S. suppliers specializing in health-care furniture.

◼ ◼ ◼

Transitions highlighted in italic

Kevin Huber can navigate through his word processing package as fast as almost any other computer user. *However*, unlike most computer users, Kevin cannot see the keyboard or his monitor. *In fact*, other than differentiating between intense light and dark shadows, Kevin sees nothing.

Legally blind [illuminates *"sees nothing"*] since birth, Kevin hears what others see thanks to adaptive technologies. *Adaptive technologies* are tools that translate visual information into audible information for visually challenged computer users.

Kevin has adjusted to his *challenge* [links this paragraph to *"challenged"* in the previous paragraph] so well that he now works as a client support representative for Microcomputer Science Centre in Mississauga, where he tests new computer technology intended for use by visually challenged individuals. He *also* shows instructors how to train persons with disabilities to compute and surf the Web using adaptive technology.

Like slanted sidewalks, or curb cuts, which are used to make streets more accessible to mobility challenged persons, adaptive technology, or electronic curb cuts, are used to make computers more accessible to physically challenged persons. [This is a transitional paragraph; we are leaving Kevin now to look at the actual technologies.]

Physical challenges can be divided into three categories: visual, hearing, and mobility. *Visual challenges* range from reduced visual acuity to blindness. *Hearing challenges* range from slight loss of hearing to deafness. And *mobility challenges* range from impaired movement of limbs to limited movement of the head and lips.

Chapter 10: Toning Up Your Writing

Tone is the attitude a writer expresses toward the subject and his or her readers. You demonstrate tone through the word and grammar choices you make and the degree of formality of your writing. The subject line, title of the document, and/or the introduction or executive summary all help establish and contribute to the overall tone.

What is the difference between the following two headlines or titles?

> **The ecological consequences of diminishing water resources in Canada.**

> **What happens when we've drained Canada dry?**

Where would you expect to find the first one? Why? Where would you expect to find the second one? Is it fair to say you might read the second one in a newspaper or magazine? Even though the subject is serious, the tone is light and informal. The headline is trying to capture the attention of a mass market—perhaps people who tend to scan the news. Notice how it plays on the name of the soft drink, Canada Dry. Look at how it uses a contraction—we've—which indicates an informal style. Consider how the title asks a question to engage the reader in a dialogue between equals.

The first title is more formal, perhaps even a bit ponderous. However, you might expect (expectation is key here) to receive a document with this headline if you were an environmental scientist reading a scholarly journal or a minister of the environment receiving a report issued by the head of one of your many departments. You don't expect to be having a conversation with the writer. Rather, you expect to sit back and be informed.

Two truths

When it comes to tone, there are two truths:

1. The tone of business writing should always be professional and meet the expectations of your readers.
2. The expectations of your readers change according to the relationship between you and the reader.

What is the difference in tone between the two e-mail messages below? Which of the two messages is more formal? Why? Which is the least formal? What are the tone indicators? What is the relationship between the sender and the receiver in each message? How does that affect tone?

> Hi Steve,
>
> Your proposal for the reply to the Johnson and Gupta request for quote is super. We just need to hammer out the production schedule. It's a tad tight right now. If we get the contract, I owe you lunch.
>
> Cheers,
> Jean

▣   ▣   ▣

> To: The Bid Committee
>
> The reply to the Johnson and Gupta Request for Quote appears complete, based on our department's evaluation. However, we have made several suggested revisions to the proposed delivery schedule to help ensure the company does not commit itself to an unrealistic production schedule.
>
> The revisions are clearly indicated in the copy of the attached report. If you have any questions or comments, please reply by September 30.

The first message, I think you would agree, is informal. Words and phrases such as *super, hammer out, tad tight,* and *owe you lunch* are informal markers, as are contractions such as *it's.* The second message is formal, as indicated by words and phrases such as *appears complete, our department's evaluation, several suggested revisions, to help ensure, are clearly indicated, the attached report,* and *please reply by.*

The writer of the first message, Jean, obviously knows the recipient, Steve. One can presume they are colleagues, perhaps even friends. The writer of the second message is representing a department that can only make suggestions; the final reply to the request for quote is up to the Bid Committee. The committee has obviously requested input, but it does not have to listen to the suggestions. In short, the tone of the second message is formal and does not take anything for granted, as in: *we have made several suggested revisions...*

Technically, there is nothing wrong with the first message; however, it is easy for email messages to be forwarded to others. You should keep that in mind when you write. While an informal tone might be appropriate when you are sending an e-mail message to a friend or to someone you've known for some time, the informal tone might not be appropriate to other readers to whom the e-mail must be forwarded. Also, e-mail messages are legal documents and considered company property. If a dispute or other legal issue occurs, your messages can be reviewed; you want to make sure you haven't said anything inappropriate and you want to ensure your tone is appropriate.

Tone: positive versus negative

Review the two sets of messages below and look at the difference the use of positive language makes to writing.

> You didn't send us your signed invoice, so we have not yet processed your payment.

> So we can process your payment promptly, please send us your signed invoice.

◼   ◼   ◼

> Your company's lack of preparation in response to the need for full financial disclosure under Sarbanes-Oxley will have a negative impact on investor confidence.

> Preparing for full financial disclosure under Sarbanes-Oxley will greatly boost investor confidence in your company.

The second message in each set uses positive language and the reader would be more likely to respond in a positive manner, as the writer intended. In other words, given the positive benefits presented in each of the second messages, the reader would be more likely to submit an invoice and would be more likely to prepare for full financial discloser.

You can use negative words and phrases—*not, have not, did not, never*—or words and phrases that convey concepts in a negative manner—*lack of, negative impact*—in business writing; however, conveying your ideas using a positive tone more often will generate the results you want. If a situation is life and death, may lead to an injury or substantial loss, or if you have not previously received the results you desired, you might have to resort to a strong, negative tone. However, in general business correspondence, you should not convey ideas, concepts, and requests using negative language. Or as one might say in a much more positive manner: *in general business correspondence, you should convey ideas, concepts, and requests using positive language.*

Sometimes language can be positive but still convey a negative tone. The passage below uses positive language; however, the tone is negative. It says, "Go away. Don't bother me. Solve this yourself."

Here's the scenario. Upon requesting information by e-mail about financial planning services from your bank, you receive the following reply:

> Your e-mail of December 5 requesting information about the bank's financial planning services has been received. Financial planning services are offered through selected branches. For information on the bank's financial planning services, you should contact someone at your local branch and find out the closest branch that offers such services.

How would you feel if you received an e-mail message from your bank like the one above? Again, the language is not negative; however, the tone is. It says, "I can't help you; I don't even want to try." On the other hand, the message below uses mostly positive words (it does spell out a negative situation but offers a positive solution) coupled with a positive and helpful tone:

> Thank you for your e-mail. Our financial planning services are offered through selected branches and I forwarded your request for information to the Roncesvalles and Howard Park branch, the branch closest to your home.
>
> You should hear from a financial advisor by Monday. If you do not hear from a financial advisor by then, or if

you have any other questions, please contact me for
assistance.

In summary, when preparing to write, assess your topic, audience and the
situation. Then strike the right tone—a tone that is appropriate to your
audience, topic, and situation—when you write.

You point of view

The use of *you* or *your* (the *you viewpoint*) can be inclusive and even friendly
(as it is in the first Johnson and Gupta e-mail message and in the second e-
mail reply from the bank). Using *you* can make the reader feel like part of
the event, situation, or even problem.

Advertisers often use *you* to make it seem like they are talking to one
reader even though the ad appears in a newspaper that will be read by
thousands of people. For years, the McDonald's slogan was "You deserve a
break today."

While *you* can be polite and inclusive, it can also feel like an accusation or
a command (in the imperative, as we've seen, the *you* is often implied). Can
you feel the difference in tone between the following?

Help me sort this out.

I need help resolving this.

Can you please help me resolve this?

While the first two lines might get you the help you need, the *you* in third
line, coupled with *please*, makes the request a personal and polite appeal for
help that will more likely help you get the help you need. Notice, though,
that the words like *you* and *your* are not used in the second Johnson and
Gupta e-mail. The e-mail message could have been written like this:

Your Johnson and Gupta proposal appears complete and
thorough, based on our department's evaluation.
Several small revisions to your document, however,
would ensure that you are not committing yourself to an
unrealistic schedule. These revisions are marked on the
copy of your report attached to this message.

The use of the you viewpoint in this manner makes it feel as if the writer
is taking an "us versus them" or "me versus you" approach to distance

himself or herself from a potential problem—as if to say "this is your problem, not mine." Instead, in the second Johnson and Gupta e-mail message, the writer is formal, professional, and polite without using *you*. The writer represents a department and is writing on behalf of that department to people who do not have to take the offered advice, but who do need to hear it before making a decision. By not using *you*, the writer is actually more engaged in the situation.

Although there are problems with the report, the writer is positive: "The Johnson and Gupta proposal appears complete and thorough..." The writer transitions to the potential problem using the word *however*. However, the writer describes the *revisions* as *small* and the word *revisions* is not modified with words such as *urgent* or *required*. The writer also presents the benefit that will follow if the revisions are made: These revisions will "ensure that the company is not committing itself to an unrealistic schedule."

Compare this way of expressing the thought versus the following:

> **"Making these revisions will ensure that you do not totally screw up the schedule."**

I admit that I have exaggerated for effect, but do you see the difference? The *you* in the above line says the problem is all yours, not mine. In other words, although *you* can be inclusive, it can also feel like a command or an accusation or distance the writer from the situation.

Ultimately, you have to decide if you will use the you viewpoint or not. And if you use it, you have to decide on how often you will use it and on the overall tone you want to establish, such as inclusionary or exclusionary, imperative, or helpful.

As I have said before, what you want to do when you are engaged in business writing is be aware of your choices and then make the choice that best helps you achieve your purpose or objective. In short, it's up to you to choose the tone you will use and to ensure it is the right tone for the situation. More often than not, as I've mentioned, you will find that the use of a positive tone will help you produce the results you desire. That does not mean you should never use a negative tone; however, make sure the tone you use suits the topic, reader, and situation.

Chapter 11: The Three Cs of Writing

Business writing should be a lot of things. Primarily, it should be focused rather than rambling. To achieve focus, you need to know

- your topic,
- your purpose, and
- your call to action.

In other words, you need to know what you are writing about, why you are writing, and what you want your reader to do. Even if you are sending a 'For Your Information' (FYI) message that does not require the reader to act, you should know before you write that you do not want the reader to do anything.

The more you know before you write, the more likely you are to communicate all you have to write to achieve your purpose and motivate the action you desire. (I am an advocate of writing this information down so you are not trying to remember it as you write.) Also, the more you know before you write, the more likely you are to instinctively use the first three Cs of communication—clarity, conciseness, and coherence. You are also more likely to achieve the other two other Cs: consistency and correctness.

Although you want to be as consistent and correct as possible when you write, consistency and correctness are more often achieved when editing a document. With that in mind, we will focus on the first three Cs in this chapter.

What exactly do the three Cs mean, and why are they important to business writing?

Conciseness, clarity, coherence

Conciseness means that you have removed extraneous words, phrases, clauses, and sentences from your writing, without sacrificing important details or clarity. In other words, your writing emphasizes and supports the most important ideas in your document—those that help the reader understand your purpose and persuade the reader to take the action you need him or her to take.

Think of achieving conciseness as packing a single carry-on bag for a three-day business trip rather than encumbering yourself with a carry-on bag, suit bag, and suitcase—all containing articles of clothing and supplies you do not need and will not use.

Clarity is essential to understanding and is important if you are to achieve your purpose. If your readers do not understand what you want them to know or do, and if they do not understand why you want them to know or do it, then your document is not clear. If your writing is concise but not clear, you will not achieve your purpose.

To extend our packing imagery, think of packing one bag for your trip but reaching your destination only to realize that you forgot to pack your deodorant or some other vital accoutrement. You packed concisely, but not clearly.

Coherence means that the relationship between all the ideas presented in your document makes sense and supports your purpose and that your document reads in a unified, focused manner, progressing logically from point to point.

In terms of luggage, imagine if you were going to Montreal in the middle of winter and you packed winter socks and sandals instead of boots, or thick sweaters and shorts instead of pants. That is illogical—or incoherent—packing.

Writing that lacks conciseness, clarity, and coherence is ineffective and can lead to business problems—or worse. Poorly written business documents can cost an organization time and money, particularly if they lead to confusion and poor decisions. As for worse? Imagine that you are giving life-saving instructions and your writing is not concise, clear, and coherent. Such writing can literally cost lives.

The backbone of clear, concise, coherent writing is planning and organization. If you invest time up front planning and getting organized, you will more likely employ the three Cs. In short, harness the writing process if you want to be an effective writer.

Or would you rather write like bureaucrats often write? Here's how a bureaucrat might write something:

> We are less than pleased due to the fact that it is, at this point in time, the season of winter.

And here is how Shakespeare wrote it:

> Now is the winter of our discontent.

I am not saying write like a Shakespeare to be effective; I am saying avoid writing in a bureaucratic manner to be effective.

When politicians deliver sentences like the one below, it may seem as if they are delivering a strong, effective statement.

> First and foremost, we will ensure that each and every Canadian from coast to coast enjoys access to basic and fundamental health care. Finally and for good, we will put this serious health-care crisis behind us.

Frankly, if you were in a great hall and listening to a brilliant speaker, the above passage might sound inspirational. It falls flat on the page, however, because it is not concise writing. Compare the above statement with the one below to see what I mean:

> By ensuring that every Canadian has access to fundamental health care, we will put the health-care crisis behind us.

Let's look at a passage that could be more concise:

> To write concisely, remove, delete, eliminate, and eradicate extraneous, superfluous, redundant words, phrases, clauses, and sentences—without sacrificing appropriate detail.

If you were to do what this passage says you should do, the revised passage would look something like this:

> To write concisely, remove redundant words, phrases, clauses, and sentences—without sacrificing appropriate detail.

On occasion, I've had people ask me if the edited passage should not look like this:

> To write concisely, remove redundant words—without
> sacrificing appropriate detail.

You want to beware of writing so concisely that you end up sacrifice meaning. Words such as "remove," "delete," "eliminate," and "eradicate" are synonyms. You only need to use one of the words to make your meaning clear. The same can be said about "extraneous," "superfluous," and "redundant." On the other hand, "words," "phrases," "clauses," and "sentences" each mean something different. Cutting any of them would cut into the clarity of your meaning.

Applying the three Cs

Let's apply what you've learned by first editing a short passage and then editing an executive summary taken from an insurance industry white paper. (A white paper is a detailed report that proposes a solution to a major issue that a company, organization, or business sector is facing.) Make both samples as clear, concise, and coherent as you can.

The insurance industry executive summary is a formal document, so the tone should be formal; however, the writing should be free of clichés and buzzwords. The document is a tad technical and I want you to rewrite it for a business audience. In other words, it is your job to sort out the business issues the executive summary addresses and then improve the document for your primary audience—senior business executives—because they are the ones who must allocate funds. Before they will allocate funds and direct Information Technology (IT) staff to implement the solution proposed in this white paper, they must grasp the business issue and the need to resolve it.

But first, here is the short passage for practice. Read it and edit it, applying the three Cs:

> Somebody has said that words are a whole lot like
> inflated money—the more of them that you use, the less
> each one of them is actually worth. Right on!
>
> Go through the executive summary that can be found
> below this here passage just as many times as it takes
> to search out, find, and annihilate all the unnecessary
> and redundant words that you can find, as well as all the
> unnecessary and redundant phrases and sentences, and
> so on. Even delete and eliminate entire paragraphs, if

required. But don't do it until after you have first and foremost completed an edit and revision of these here paragraphs!

Once you have edited the passage above, continue to read.

Note: At the end of this chapter, you will find edited versions of the above passage and of the executive summary. Edit the above passage and the executive summary before you read the suggested revisions.

Executive summary exercise

Read the executive summary below and edit it, applying the three Cs. You may want to read it several times and highlight the ideas and passages you want to keep. You can even go so far as to turn your highlighting into an outline that you will follow before you start to revise the passage.

In the face of amplified and increased competition and more intense rivalries, and in a climate of ongoing mergers and acquisitions and closer regulatory scrutiny than ever before, the life insurance industry is facing a myriad of operational, customer service, distribution channel, and competitive pressures that can lead to the failure of companies.

The Information Technology (IT) departments in life insurance companies are expected to keep a really tight lid on spending while delivering innovative solutions that increase productivity, improve customer service, and open distribution channels.

At the same time, due to increases in mergers and acquisitions, most life insurance companies are running multiple IT administration systems that often do not communicate and interface with each other.

New replacement IT systems and IT conversion projects are often cost-prohibitive; however, multiple administration system environments are crippling the industry's ability to keep a lid on operational costs and keep expenses down, and they are impairing the opportunity to implement new customer service models that are so needed in today's increasingly competitive environment.

The end result of all of this is that IT departments are under greater and increasing pressure to preserve the investment in existing or legacy systems while somehow figuring out a way to provide customer-centric life insurance service delivery solutions. In addition, they need to deliver IT methods of allowing companies to work more productively, effectively, and efficiently with life insurance distributors who are dazed and confused by the myriad of IT administrative systems mixes out there.

Under such circumstance, what the heck is an unfortunate life insurance company to do?

Faced with these challenges, insurance companies need to adopt consolidation architecture. To put it as simply as possible, a consolidation architecture is a common, centralized interface that streamlines business processes through access to, and manipulation of, consolidated and standardized customer data across multiple administrative systems.

It's like having your cake and eating it too as a consolidation architecture preserves the existing legacy IT systems while facilitating their ability to communicate with each other. New programs developed for consumers or distributors (agents) can run on any system and be fully integrated.

Revised short passage

Do not be concerned if your revised short passage is not exactly like the revised passage below. There is a degree of subjectivity to any writing.

Compare your revision to the one below and use it to help you determine if your revision is as clear, concise, and coherent as it could be. Or, frankly, use your revision to determine if the one below is as clear, concise, and coherent as it could be.

> Someone once said that words are like inflated money—the more you use, the less each one is worth. Review the executive summary below and remove redundant words, phrases, sentences, and even paragraphs if necessary. However, don't do it until you have edited this paragraph.

◼   ◼   ◼

Revised executive summary

As with the paragraph revision exercise, do not be concerned if your revised executive summary is not like the revised passage below. Compare your revision to the one below to help you determine if your revision is as clear, concise, and coherent as it could be.

> In the face of increased competition, and in a climate of mergers and acquisitions and closer regulatory scrutiny, the life insurance industry faces numerous operational, customer service, and distribution channel pressures that need to be alleviated if companies are to succeed.

> Life insurance Information Technology (IT) departments are expected to control spending while delivering solutions that increase productivity, improve customer service, and open channels to distributors (agents). However, due to mergers and acquisitions, most life insurance companies now run multiple IT administration systems that often do not communicate with each other, preventing IT staff from achieving these goals.

> The ideal solution would be to replace existing IT systems with new ones. However, this is cost-

prohibitive. Therefore, IT needs to preserve existing systems while providing solutions that enable life insurance companies to better serve customers and work more effectively with distributors.

Faced with these challenges, IT needs to adopt a cost-effective consolidation architecture—a centralized interface that allows multiple systems to communicate with each other.

With consolidation systems in place, IT can preserve legacy technology and streamline business processes across multiple systems. New business solutions, developed for consumers and distributors, can then be integrated with any system in the company.

Chapter 12: Positive; Purpose

As a freelance writer and business-writing trainer, I have to send the occasional bill collection message to clients. When I send an e-mail message, approximately forty days after sending an invoice that was due in thirty days, what do you think my purpose is?

"To get paid" is partially correct because I want to be paid. However, I also want to maintain my relationship with the client. If the tone of my e-mail message is negative, accusatory, and unprofessional, I might receive prompt payment; however, I would probably lose the client. If my first message accuses the client of willful nonpayment and if I threaten to send in a collection agency or to take the client to small claims court, the client might pay me, but why would the client want to work with me again?

When it comes to writing negative correspondence, you want to be as professional and positive as possible—especially if you are writing your first letter of complaint about a particular problem or sending your first collection letter to a tardy client. That is why I let the client know that I am following up on an invoice. I ask the client if he received the invoice or has any questions. Usually, the client replies with an apology and says the check is in the mail (and it is) or that accounting misplaced the invoice and the check will be processed in a few days or as part of the next check run.

I monitor the situation and, if the check does not arrive, follow up a few weeks later with a bit more urgency—still using a positive tone. I do not escalate the situation until it becomes obvious that the client is stonewalling, does not intend to pay, or is trying to escape his or her obligations by suggesting that I did not deliver the contracted services.

In almost every case, the check is delivered shortly after the first e-mail message. So I get paid and I maintain the relationship with the client.

If circumstances—such as repeated nonpayment of a bill—force you to escalate your requests, you still want to remain professional and avoid negative statements. At the same time, you must also clearly state your purpose and the actions you will take if the offending party remains in noncompliance. It is much like walking a fine line—you want to get from point A to point B while maintaining your balance. I am not saying you should never resort to small claims court or a collecting agency. I am saying that until you no longer want to maintain the business relationship, you have to be as clear as possible while avoiding the use of negative, accusatory, or derogatory language.

Why avoid negatives?

Negative writing often inspires a negative or defensive response. Emotionally loaded language, which negative language is, can lead to an emotional reaction rather than a logical, business-like reply. Instead of achieving your purpose, you can start a fight when you take a negative approach to communication. If you have ever posted on Internet discussion forums, you have probably seen flame wars erupt over perceived injustices. That can also happen when two parties are communicating over money or during any circumstances when the business or emotional stakes are high. In fact, if I may digress, if the financial, business, or emotional stakes are high, you might want to phone or visit the other party, as outlined in an article on my blog, "When it really matters, face-to-face matters," (www.paullima.com/blog/?p=204).

The point is, you are in business. You need to stay focused on your purpose and present your case in a clear and logical manner if you want to achieve it. The use of negative language can lead to an emotional reaction. In addition, the use of negatives or double negatives (even if not emotionally negative), can be confusing. Review the negative and positive examples below. As a reader, which message would you prefer to receive, the negative or the positive one?

> When the error message does not indicate data transmission, then the back-up function should not be used.

> The back-up function should be used only when the error message indicates data transmission.

◼   ◼   ◼

90

> We are withholding your shipment because we have not received your payment.

> We will ship your order as soon as we receive your payment.

I think it is fair to say the second statement in each of the above examples—the statements that use positive language—would be preferable. The positive statement in the first example is clear. In the second example, presenting the benefit (payment, which is positive) can motivate a positive action. At the same time, using positive language when you should clearly spell out a negative business situation can be deceptive.

> In the first quarter of this year, employee exposure to airborne lead was within 10% of acceptable health standards.

In the above example, the company is trying to put a positive spin on a negative situation, but is coming across as deceptive. Fact is, the company did not meet acceptable standards and should say so.

> In the first quarter of this year, employee exposure to airborne lead was 10% below acceptable health standards.

There are times when you should use negative language. If a situation is life and death or may lead to injury, if you have not received the results you desired after several attempts, or if someone has you so frustrated that you are willing to end your business relationship, you might resort to a negative tone. For instance, I'd suggest a sign that says, "Danger. Do not touch!" next to an electric fence is more appropriate than one that says, "Touching may result in injury."

Start with purpose

Although you want to keep your writing appropriately positive, you also want to work your purpose into the opening of any document—from a simple e-mail message to a major report. Doing so ensures that the reader reads all that follows with your purpose in mind.

On occasion, people tell me that starting with purpose feels impolite. My reply? Negative language can be impolite. Starting with purpose is effective. For instance, the message below may seem polite, but is it effective?

> How are you? Hope all is well and that you are not too busy. I need your feedback on the environmental report ASAP so I can submit it. Hey, maybe we can do lunch next week?

If you start with your purpose, you are more inclined to write:

> We need to submit the attached environmental report to the ministry by the end of the month so we can obtain funding. Your feedback is required before the report can be submitted. Please provide feedback by April 21.

Let's say that an earlier request was ignored. If that is the case, you might want to be more emphatic and spell out negative consequences of inaction, but you still want to keep your overall tone positive. In other words, avoid accusations.

> As previously mentioned, the attached environmental report must be submitted to the ministry by the end of the month or we will not obtain funding from the province. Your feedback is required by April 21 before the report can be submitted.

As the reader of either message, I know why you are writing (to get my feedback on the attached report), what I have to do, why I have to do it (the benefits of doing it in the first message; the consequence of not doing it in the second), and when I have to do it by. How effective is that? And if the consequential stakes are higher, don't pull your punches, or *be as explicit as required*, I might say if I wanted to eliminate the negative "don't." For instance, if your company will go bankrupt if you don't get funding, say so.

Note on ASAP

By the way, if you think your message would be more effective if you said that you need feedback *ASAP*, think again. Avoid using "ASAP" or even "as soon as possible" in e-mail or any other correspondence. While ASAP means the same thing, according to the dictionary, to you and the reader, it does not mean the same thing, according to the calendar, to you and the reader. You might want an action completed by Wednesday afternoon, but if you use ASAP, the reader may look at his schedule and decide that Friday morning is as soon as he can complete the action.

If you say something like, "Please return the report with your comments by noon on April 21" and you don't get the report by noon of that day, you can follow up by e-mail or by phone. If you say, "Please return the report with you comments ASAP" you don't have a firm follow-up date. So be as specific as possible. Being specific about your purpose and any deadlines related to achieving your purpose actually helps you help the reader help you.

Purpose eliminates mystery

When you are writing formal business documents, you are not writing mystery novels. The reader should not have to unravel your purpose. Instead, you should lead with your purpose. For instance, say you want to inquire about leasing cars for your company from an automotive company. Presumably, your purpose would be to receive a quote from the company. Based on your purpose, organize the following sentences so that you are starting with purpose. When you are done, you should have an outline for an opening paragraph:

1.   General Engines has an excellent reputation for reliable service.
2.   We're looking for the best lease price, coupled with reliable service.
3.   We would like to receive a quote on the lease of four XK4s.
4.   Call us by October 30 to discuss our needs, before issuing the quote.
5.   We would like to do business with the local dealer.

> **Place the points in order, starting with your purpose, before you read on.**

Imagine if you had the above five points in front of you before you started to write. What you would do next is

- decide which of the points you should address;
- decide which, if any, you should not address; and
- organize the points you want to address in terms of where you should start, what you should write next, and so on.

At that point, it's all over but the writing. Write from point to point and you are done. That is the power of organization, no matter what type of document you are writing. Being able to jot down the points you need to address (creating your outline) comes from research or knowing what you need to say to accomplish your purpose.

With that in mind, here is my suggested order, starting with purpose:

1. We would like to receive a quote on the lease of four XK4s.
2. We're looking for the best lease price, coupled with reliable service.
3. General Engines has an excellent reputation for reliable service.
4. We would like to do business with the local dealer.
5. Call us by October 30 to discuss our needs, before issuing a quote.

If I am the leasing manager and I receive this inquiry, I will start thinking about how I can help you—how I can meet your purpose—based on the first point. But what if the leasing manager has moved to the parts department and you don't know it? If I am the former leasing manager, I will open your e-mail message and, based on your first point, I will redirect it to the appropriate person at the dealership.

Again, by starting with purpose, you help the reader help you. Not only is your purpose more likely to be met, you are saving the reader time. He does not have to spend time wondering what your e-mail is about. And once you have your points in order, you write. So you might convert your points to a letter like this:

> Dear Mr. Lease Manager:
>
> ABC Inc. is looking to receive a quote on the lease of four XK4s. We are interested in the best lease price, coupled with reliable service, <u>for which General Engines has an excellent reputation</u>.
>
> We would like to receive a quote from your local dealer. Please call us by October 30 to discuss our needs in detail, before issuing the quote.

I am not saying the above paragraph represents your entire letter. Depending on your relationship with the company, you might want to give the dealership some background information about your organization. If you are putting out a formal tender, you might want to direct the reader to an attachment or an enclosed document. What I am saying is that if you put your purpose first, there are times when you might not have to say much of anything else. And if you do have to write more, at least your reader is reading with *your purpose* in mind.

Notice that I have underlined this phrase: "for which General Engines has an excellent reputation" in the letter. I call such phrases window dressing. They may be nice to write, but they do not advance your cause. So why use them? There is no reason to do so; if you cut the phrase, it would not be missed. In fact, I suggest that you cut such phrases when you are creating your formal outline.

Am I adamantly opposed to window dressing? Let me answer the question with a question: How does it help you? If you have one window-dressing phrase in a letter or an e-mail message, it most likely will not interfere with your communication. If you have one or two window-dressing phrases every paragraph or two, however, your document will not be as clear, concise, or coherent as it could be, and should be. That will interfere with the effectiveness of your communication.

Purpose exercise

Let's do another purpose exercise. Review the sentences below. Your purpose is to have the recipient of your message send you a copy of a presentation delivered at the NACB convention. Pick the sentence that *best states your purpose*. You don't have to put all the sentences in order; just pick the one that best states your purpose.

1. I heard good things about the speech you presented on March 15 at the NACB convention.
2. Several managers in my firm have asked me to write you regarding your speech at NACB.
3. Our consulting firm would like to obtain a copy of the speech you gave at the NACB convention last week so we can circulate it to clients.
4. As you may know, our company deals with some of the issues you raised recently in your speech at the NACB convention.
5. Do you give or sell people copies of your presentations, like the one you recently delivered at NACB

Pick the sentence that best states your purpose, before reading on.

When I conduct workshops based on this book, 95% of the participants pick the third sentence as the one that best states purpose, and I agree with them. Many participants also say that they would not start their letter with that statement, and I don't have a problem with that.

As you know, I have been saying that you should start with purpose. I want to make it clear, however, that you do not have to state your purpose in your opening sentence. You need to define your purpose clearly so you can convey it clearly. But you also have to determine if your purpose sentence will be your opening sentence, middle sentence, or the final sentence of your opening paragraph. In other words, you have some latitude—as long as you work your purpose (consider it your topic sentence) into your opening paragraph.

With that in mind, your opening paragraph could read something like this:

> I heard good things from my staff about the speech you presented on March 15 at the NACB convention. As you may know, our company deals with some of the issues you raised in your speech. We would like to obtain a copy of the speech you gave at the conference that we might be able to circulate to clients. We are willing to discuss any fee that may be associated with this.

Notice that our purpose is the second last sentence. The reader does not personally know the writer, so there is nothing wrong with providing a bit of background information before hitting the purpose statement. The writer knows that some people who give presentations often sell them to companies, so right after he conveys his purpose the writer overcomes any objection the reader might have by ensuring that the reader knows the writer is willing to pay for the speech. So the writer has captured attention, held interest, influenced attitude—all in one paragraph. And the writer has all but asked for action.

If the reader gives away copies of speeches, he can say so. If the reader sells copies of speeches, he can let the writer know what the cost will be. At the same time, if the writer is not willing to pay for a copy of the speech, the writer should not use the last sentence.

The point is this: Do you see how much you can pack into a paragraph when you think about what you want to say, and write in a clear, concise, and coherent manner? Such writing stems from knowing your purpose and organizing your thoughts before you write.

Exceptions? Not really, but sort of...

I once gave a workshop based on this book to a group of teachers who resisted my "start with purpose" message. When they returned from summer vacation, they had a lot of business information to communicate with each other, yet they felt it was rude to not ask other teachers how their holidays were when communicating for the first time after coming back from holidays. I made three suggestions:

- Send a "hello, how are you, how were your holidays" e-mail separate from any business e-mail messages to get the informal message out of your system.

- If you don't have time for that or feel it might add to the general e-mail clutter, open your first business message with a one-line paragraph: "Welcome back. Hope you enjoyed your holidays." Make sure your purpose is clearly stated in the next paragraph. The paragraph separation helps the reader separate the short personal message from the business message.

- Open with your purpose. Write the body of your message, including any action statement. Include a short personal message as a separate paragraph at the end of your message. Perhaps something like this: "I look forward to hearing about your holidays when we meet in the staff room."

I am not asking you to be unfriendly or rude. I am asking you to be effective and efficient. If you are clear, you are more likely to be understood and achieve your objective. So stay focused on the business issue. If it helps, before you write ask yourself this question: what is the consequence of being misunderstood and not accomplishing my objective?

If there are absolutely no consequences, you might ask yourself if you even need to send the message. If there are minor or major consequences, you will—I presume—want to be as clear as possible and not muddy your business writing with personal statements.

Soft entry

The teachers had another issue, one that I can imagine anyone in customer service having or, frankly, anyone who has to write about a delicate subject.

The teachers wanted what they described as a "soft entry" into writing difficult e-mail messages, messages about negative issues that had to be sent to the parents of students. I stressed the need to clearly define purpose and allude to it in the subject line so they could capture the attention of the parents. In other words, even if a message is negative, you do not want to keep your reader in suspense. However, that does not mean you slap your reader across the face.

The need for a "soft entry" comes from the fact that defining purpose can be difficult. For instance, a teacher described the following scenario:

> What if a good student goes bad? One day he gets into an argument with another student. Another day he falls asleep in class. These would be dealt with by the teacher; the parents would not need to be notified. Then the student sets off firecrackers at the back of the class. This is something for which he could be suspended and, of course, the parents would have to be notified. Do I start my e-mail with "Dear Parents: Your son set off firecrackers in class today and may be suspended"?

My answer: Define your *true* purpose. To help you do that, ask yourself what the parents know and what the parents need to know. For instance, based on previous reports, the parents know their son is well behaved and gets good marks. The parents don't know about the behavioral shift. So the purpose is not to notify the parents that the student could be suspended. The true purpose is to notify the parents of the shift in behavior and your concern. The action the teacher wants is to set up a meeting, but that is not the purpose.

Watch how we can have a soft entry that states our purpose. In other words, there is no need to start with "how are you and how are things?" (which would be silly under the circumstances).

Below, I present the full e-mail we developed. Notice how we allude to our purpose in the subject line and make it clear in our opening paragraph. In short, by the end of the first paragraph, we have achieved our purpose, which is to express concern over the student's shift in behavior.

By the end of the e-mail, we have asked for action based on our purpose. In between, we let the parents know that suspension is an option (not that it will happen), so we have even spelled out the consequences that could occur (not an overt threat) if there is no return to proper deportment.

Subject: Shift in Tommy's behavior at school

Dear Mr. and Mrs. Smith,

As you know, Tommy has been an excellent student who gets great marks. Recently, his behavior has started to change and we are concerned. Last week, he initiated an argument with another student and he fell asleep in class. Yesterday, he set off firecrackers at the back of the class.

We did not notify you of the first two incidents because they were minor and Tommy promised to settle down. However, the firecracker incident is serious. Students can be suspended for engaging in such behavior.

Before we take any action whatsoever, we need to meet with you to discuss the situation in detail. For instance, there may extenuating circumstances of which we are not aware. Can you please notify me in the next day or two when you will be able to meet after school? I look forward to your call or e-mail.

Notice that by clearly defining purpose you can allude to it in the subject line and state it in the first paragraph. In addition, we have a soft, but appropriate, opening line. Following your purpose—expressing your concern over the shift in Tommy's behavior—you give the parents appropriate background information that keeps them interested and influences their attitude. Then you state your call to action.

A couple of teachers said they would prefer to phone the parents rather than send an e-mail. I have no problem with that and, in this case, I'd encourage it. However, before making such a call you would still want to organize your thoughts and compose the message you want to convey. If you called, you would identify yourself and ask if the parent you reached had a moment to talk. Then you would essentially deliver the message above and let the parent respond. In other words, you would still convey your purpose, your reason for calling, up front.

From purpose to conclusion

Of course you have to do more than start with purpose. You have to write from purpose to conclusion. That is where answering the W5 questions, and creating a detailed outline, come into play. Asking the W5 questions and creating your outline—all the points you want to make, in the order you should make them—will enable you to write from purpose to conclusion, as in the example below.

> **Subject**: Meeting to discuss pricing concerns
>
> Hi Chris,
>
> I would like to meet to discuss some concerns over the recent proposal to increase the price of widgets you supply to Acme Manufacturing.
>
> Retailers such as Floor-Mart are exerting pressures on margins and I would like to reach a pricing arrangement with you before we place our fourth quarter order in August.
>
> I am available to meet the week of June 18 to discuss your proposal. I will call you on Wednesday to set up a date, time, and location for the meeting. If you have any questions, please email or call me.

The purpose is to meet about a specific issue, so it is no surprise that we see the word "meeting" in the subject line and we see the word "meet" in the opening paragraph. But we also quickly see the reason for the meeting—pricing concerns. That is an attention-grabbing concern that will get the reader thinking about agreeing to meet. With that in mind, let's practice defining your true business purpose and putting your purpose first.

Practice putting purpose first

Keeping positive writing, where appropriate, in mind, I want you to read the following short case studies. When you finish reading each case, jot down your purpose and the action you would like the reader to take. Ask yourself: What is my true business purpose? What do I want to achieve? Why? What action would I like to see the reader take?

Case Study One: Hotel

On business trips to London, Ontario, you stay at the Chelsea Hotel. On your most recent trip, conditions were below expected standards. The room was not clean, and dining room service was poor. In addition, the rates had been increased 5%. You travel to London every quarter on business. Your company has used this hotel for several years because it is conveniently located and, even with the recent price increase, offers reasonable rates.

◼   ◼   ◼

Case Study Two: Furniture

On November 1, you ordered furniture from the Office Company catalogue. Your order arrived on November 7, but two chairs were missing. You called and spoke to Harry who said he would take care of it. On November 11, one chair arrived; it was the wrong color. You called and found out that Harry had quit. Nobody else knew about your problem. The person you talked to asked you to e-mail the manager.

Once you have written down your purpose, and the actions you would like to see each reader take, compose opening paragraphs for each of the case studies. (You can review sample openings for each case study at the end of this chapter.)

> **Determine your business purpose for each case study and write an opening paragraph that includes your purpose, before you read the paragraphs at the end of the chapter.**

Continue your purpose practice

The next two exercises have you writing letters that address negative situations. At first blush, it might look like you have to write a collection letter for one of the case studies below and a letter of complaint for the other. However, there is a catch. The case studies give you insight into both sides of the same issue. The hope is that by seeing that there are at least two sides to this issue (there are always at least two sides to issues) you will be able to write concise, coherent, focused letters that state your case in a professional, positive, logical manner. You might even see that your purpose is not to write collection and complaint letters. To begin the exercise, read the two case studies below before you write.

Case Study A: Trinket Ltd.'s issue

Widgets are a main component used in the manufacturing of your product, trinkets. For the last year, you have been ordering widgets in bulk—25,000 units per month—from Widget Inc.

Widget ships you 25,250 units on a just-in-time basis but only charges you for 25,000 because there is an agreed upon possible fault level of up to 1%. (This arrangement is common in manufacturing.)

Widget Inc.'s prices are competitive. You pay 50% down ($10,000) and the balance two weeks after delivery. If your payment is late, as it has been three times in the past year due to the installation of a new accounting system, you are charged a 2% late fee on the next invoice. However, Widget waived the penalty fee twice.

You have had a solid business relationship with Widget Inc. (You are not friends with your counterpart. You met him twice—once for lunch when negotiating the deal and once at a Chamber of Commerce meeting.)

In the first four months, two of Widget's shipments were several hours late, causing you minor production delays, but the delivery issues have been resolved. However, your last shipment was short (24,950 widgets were shipped) and the fault level was high (1.5%), leaving you with 24,575 widgets.

Although you had surplus widgets from previous shipments, you were not able to cover all your orders, which were higher than expected. In the end, you short-shipped trinkets to your major client, Floor-Mart. Floor-Mart sent you an angry e-mail, threatening to find another supplier, and invoked a penalty clause in your contract, which cost you 5% ($5,000) on a $100,000 invoice.

You have decided to withhold the final payment on the last batch of widgets until you have resolved the issue with Widget Inc. You are now going to write a letter to your counterpart of Widget Inc.

You are the CEO of Trinket Ltd., the top cheese, not an accounting manager or clerk. Write a letter to the CEO of Widget Inc.

Note: Before you write, determine your business purpose and the action you want to see the reader take. Write a business letter, using an appropriate tone, meant to achieve your purpose. Include your purpose in your opening paragraph.

◼   ◼   ◼

Case Study B: Widget Inc.'s issue

Widgets are an important component used in the manufacturing of trinkets. For the last year, Trinket Ltd. has been ordering widgets in bulk—25,000 units per month—from your company.

You ship 25,250 units on a just-in-time basis but only charge for 25,000 as there is a fault level of up to 1%. Trinket understands and accepts this fault level.

Your products are competitively priced. Trinket Ltd. pays 50% down ($10,000) and the balance two weeks after delivery. If payment is late, as it has been three times, you charge a 2% fee on the next invoice. However, as a good will gesture, you waived the late fee the first two times payments were late.

You have had a solid business relationship with your counterpart at Trinket. (You are not friends with your counterpart. You met him twice—once for lunch when negotiating the deal and once at a Chamber of Commerce meeting.)

Early on, you shipped two orders several hours late, causing Trinket Manufacturing minor production delays. You thought you had resolved delivery issues; however, your last shipment of widgets was short (24,950 widgets were shipped) and the fault level was high (1.5%), due to machine repair problems caused by a third-party maintenance company. You were not concerned because you believed Trinket Ltd. had surplus widgets from previous shipments to cover its orders.

Your accounts receivable clerk received a call from the Trinket accounts payable clerk explaining that Trinket was unable to cover all its orders. Trinket's major client,

Floor-Mart, is threatening to find another trinket supplier and has invoked a penalty clause, which cost Trinket $5,000.

Trinket's payment is overdue. You are now going to write a letter to your counterpart at Trinket.

You are the CEO of Widget Inc., the top cheese, not an accounting manager or clerk. Write a letter to the CEO of Trinket Ltd.

Note: Before you write, determine your business purpose and the action you want to see the reader take. Write a business letter, using an appropriate tone, meant to achieve your purpose. Include your purpose in your opening paragraph.

I recommend that you do your preparation work and outline the points you will address in your letters, in the order in which you will address them. To help you organize your thoughts, answer the following W5 questions:

- Who did what to whom, when, and where?
- What was the consequence?
- Why did this happen (if known)?
- Why are you writing? (What is your business purpose?)
- What action do you want to see take place? Who should take action? When and where? Why?

I suggest you write no more than five to seven paragraphs per letter and make sure that you make your business purpose is clearly stated in your opening paragraphs. Use the proper tone in relation to the message and your audience—CEO to CEO. Write well-organized, clear, concise, coherent, focused letters. End with conclusions that spell out what action you plan to take or expect the recipient to take—who does what by when, where and/or how?

> **Determine your business purpose for each case study. Write your letters before you read the Widget and Trinket letters at the end of the chapter.**

◨ ◨ ◨

Hotel case study sample leads

I want to stress one last time the importance of defining your true business purpose before you write. The purpose, as you define it, directly influences the words you write, the tone you use, and any action you request.

For instance, in the hotel case study, you had to write an opening paragraph to the manager of the Chelsea Hotel in London, Ontario. You had a negative experience at the hotel; however, you use the hotel on a quarterly basis because it is conveniently located and offers reasonable rates. So what is your purpose? Do you want a full or partial refund? Or do you want assurance that the problems will be fixed before you book your next business trip?

If you are angry and want a full refund, here's what you might write:

> I stayed at your hotel last week and was extremely unhappy with the service. The food was cold, the room was a mess, and some of your staff members were rude. I am not at all satisfied and would like a full refund ASAP.

I am *not* suggesting the above passage is solid, or even proper, business writing, but it does convey a particular purpose. However, if you said that your purpose was to obtain a refund, I'd suggest you might want to think again. From the case study: "You travel to London every quarter on business. Your company has used this hotel for several years because it is conveniently located and... offers reasonable rates." With that in mind, how would you feel if you obtained a refund and the service did not improve the next time you were there? What would you have achieved? So I repeat: determine your *true* business purpose before you write.

If you want assurance that the problems will be fixed before you book your next business trip, this is what you might write:

> Last week I stayed at your hotel and encountered several service-related issues. Due to business in London, I had planned to stay at your hotel once a month over the next year. However, I need your assurance that service levels will improve before I commit to doing so.

In workshops, people have asked me if they can ask for assurance that conditions will improve *and* a refund. First off, what is your primary purpose? Do you want to find a new, more expensive, less conveniently located hotel? What happens if the manager grants you a refund but conditions are just as poor the next time you are there? What happens if the manager does not give you a refund?

The fact is, by asking for two things—a refund and improved conditions—you muddy the water. Instead of assuring you that conditions were improved, the manager might fight your request for a refund. That may be a sign of a poor manager, but that is not your issue—not if your primary business purpose is to be assured that conditions at the hotel have improved.

In short, you want to determine your true business purpose and focus on that. (For instance, if you were a consumer who had stayed at the hotel in a resort area during a vacation and had experienced poor service and poor conditions, I could understand if you asked for a refund. That purpose makes sense.)

For the sake of argument, let's say you disagree with the purpose I am suggesting. I have no real problem with that. In other words, if you decide that your business purpose is to obtain a refund, I am not going to say, "No, you are wrong" (although I honestly don't think that asking for a refund is the best business response). What I am going to say is this: Understand that you will write a different letter, based on your purpose, than I will write based on mine. That is the point of this exercise, to understand that purpose influences the words you use, the tone you use, and the action you request.

◘   ◘   ◘

Furniture case study sample lead

Here is a possible lead for the furniture case study letter:

> I hope you can resolve a problem with my furniture order. On November 1, I ordered office furniture from the Office Company catalogue, but two chairs were missing when my order arrived. I called to sort this out and, on November 11, I received one additional chair; however, it was the wrong color. The person I talked to about my order no longer works for you and no one seems to know about my problem. I would like you to sort this out for me by the end of the week.

I have chosen to open this letter with my purpose—to get help solving the problem. Then I give some background information (because the recipient is not familiar with my problem) and end with a stronger purpose statement, one that includes a deadline.

Even though I have included a deadline, I do not spell out any consequences, such as: "I would like you to sort this out for me by the end of the week or I will return all the furniture that I have purchased at your store." If the manager does not call and assure me the problem will be sorted out, I can escalate my complaint and include consequences.

The letter would, of course, continue beyond the first paragraph to include additional background information, such as the invoice number and model numbers of the chairs that did not arrive. I would end by reiterating my call to action and include my phone number and e-mail address.

By providing a deadline—the end of the week—I know that I can follow up by a specific time and escalate the complaint, if the issue is not resolved.

There are other ways to word the opening paragraph, but what I want to reiterate is this: if you want to capture the attention of your reader off the top, include your purpose in your opening paragraph.

If you wanted to include a shorter deadline in your letter—say you needed the furniture sooner for a particular business reason—I would have no problem with that. The point is, you have to think about what you need and why you need it before you write, so you can write a clear, concise, coherent, focused message that starts with your purpose, establishes an appropriate tone, includes relevant background information, adjusts the attitude of the reader, and includes a clear and appropriate call to action.

Sample letter from Trinket to Widget

Below I've set up the sample letter from Trinket to Widget using the standard full block style (letterhead, double space between paragraphs; no paragraph indent). Notice how the purpose is clearly stated in the opening paragraph and the body of the letter provides background information required to support the purpose but does not rehash old issues that have been resolved. The tone is positive, and the concluding paragraph states who will do what next and when. The action reinforces the writer's purpose.

Trinket Ltd.
123 ABC Street, Toronto, Ontario A1B 2C3
(416) 555-1212 - www.trinket.com

March 16, 2009

Mr. Tom Kohl
Chief Executive Officer
Widget Inc.
501 City Drive
Mississauga, Ontario M1P 3G0

Dear Mr. Kohl:

Re: Resolving problem with shipment of widgets

We require your assistance in resolving a recent shipment problem. Our last order of widgets from Widget Inc. was short shipped and had a higher than normal fault rate and we need your assurance this will not occur again.

The shortage came at a busy time for Trinket Ltd. and we were unable to fill all our orders. Although we had surplus widgets, we did not have enough to compensate for the short shipment and the increased fault rate.

Floor-Mart, our largest customer, was upset by the shortage of trinkets and has threatened to take its business elsewhere. If that happens, both our companies will lose significant business. In an effort to ensure that this problem does not occur again, we must receive your assurance that:
  • future orders will be shipped in full
  • quality control issues will be addressed.

Trinket Ltd. and Widget Inc. have had a strong business relationship over the last year, one that we hope to continue developing.

Once we have your assurance about future shipments, we would like to arrange a meeting to discuss the outstanding accounting issues, which I am confident we can resolve so that we can continue our mutually profitable relationship. I will follow up with a phone call to set up the meeting. In the meantime, if you have any questions, please contact me.

Sincerely,
Sharon Selma
Chief Executive Officer

◼   ◼   ◼

Sample letter from Widget to Trinket

The purpose in the letter below is clear: to assure Trinket that the issue has been resolved. Notice, however, how the letter starts with an apology and that there is no attempt by Widget to blame the third-party maintenance company. There is also an effort to sort out the invoice issue. It won't simply go away by itself, so it must be addressed. The concluding paragraph restates the apology and invites Trinket to call if there are any questions.

Dear Ms. Selma:

Re: Resolving under-shipment of widgets

Please accept my apologies for the under-shipment of widgets, and the higher than normal fault rate, in our last order. Quality is important to Widget and I want to assure you that we have identified and fixed our recent manufacturing problem. We can now guarantee that we will be shipping full orders with acceptable fault levels.

I also want you to know that we will now maintain a surplus inventory of widgets. Should a problem occur, we will be able to ship your full order. Should you require a rush order of additional widgets, we will be able to accommodate you.

Once again, I would like to apologize for the shipment issue and hope to continue supplying high-quality widgets to Trinket Manufacturing.

We will adjust your invoice to reflect the short shipment and will deducted the cost of all faulty widgets. Please contact me by the end of the week if you have any questions concerning this.

Sincerely,
Tom Kohl
CEO
Widget Inc.

Chapter 13: E-mail Etiquette & Replies

We have looked at writing e-mail messages using the W5 (who, what, where, when, and why) process as an effective shortcut to the business-writing process. However, I want to spend a bit of time looking at replying to e-mail messages and some basic e-mail writing etiquette.

Replying to e-mail messages

When writing e-mail messages, you want to at least allude to your purpose in the subject line and make your purpose clear in the opening paragraph. But does that rule hold true when replying to an e-mail message? Absolutely. When someone communicates with you, you still have to determine your purpose before you reply. Your purpose might be something as simple as to inform the writer that you can do what was requested. If so, that's what you want to let the writer know.

There may be times when your reply is more complicated than a simple "Yes, I can do what you requested by the date you need it." If that is the case, use your W5 to create your reply outline. In other words, think before you reply:

- Who are you and to whom are you writing?
- What is your relationship?
- What are you writing about?
- Why are you writing?
- What objections, if any, do you anticipate?
- (How) do you overcome them, if required?
- What do you need done, or need to do, if anything? When and where?

After you answer the W5 questions, outline and prioritize your points. Make the points you want to make through clear, concise, focused writing.

Review the points you made, compared to your original W5 answers. Edit and revise as may be necessary. Proofread. Click and send.

Are there ways to shorten the process when replying? Considering that it might take you only a moment or two to go through the process, I'd suggest that you not take any shortcuts. If you leave out any important information, the entire process will take more time than it should because the person you replied to will have to ask for clarification and you'll have to reply again. Or the person you replied to will misunderstand your message and something important might fall through the cracks.

Adding to the reply process

In fact, I'd like to add to the process. When I receive an important or complex e-mail message, I copy it, hit reply, and paste it in the reply box. I reread it and then outline my W5 below the message I've pasted into the reply space.

Once that is done, I write my reply by editing the original message— eliminating anything that I do not have to address and revising anything I need to reply to. In short, I use the original message as a template for my reply. It's as if the original message is a stone block from which I sculpt my reply. But I also make sure I outline my W5 so that I can add information, as may be required, as I reply to the original message. Of course, before I hit send, I review my reply and make any necessary edits.

There is a certain irony here: the better written the original message is, the more effective my reply is. In other words, if the original message is effective and comprehensive, I tend not to have to pull in anything from my W5 work. With that in mind, allow me to summarize this reply process:

- Read the original message.
- Copy the original message.
- Hit reply (you will see the original message below an *original message* line).
- Paste the copied original message above the original message line.
- Jot down answers to W5, in relation to the original message, beneath the original message.
- Sculpt your reply out of the original message, including any pertinent details from your W5 points.
- Edit/proofread your reply and send.

Note: This method may not work for Blackberries, iPhones and other smart phones. However, the same principle applies: Make sure you respond to the salient points raised in the original message while adding additional points based on your W5 thinking.

Avoid the >> reply

Why do I copy the original message and then compose over it, instead of simply replying to various elements of the original message under those elements?

One of your goals in writing is to be clear. When you reply to various elements of a message by writing under each of those elements, clarity can suffer. Imagine if a message goes back and forth several times and both writers reply below lines in the original message. Soon you could be looking at a message like this:

> \> I agree with what you're saying, and believe
> \> we can work together to resolve the issue.
> \> I too have a few concerns about who should
> \> take the lead on this one. Let's kick it up the
> \> ladder and see what Tom thinks.

> \>> This is something that needs to be resolved
> \>> quickly if we are going to avoid serious issues
> \>> down the road with our staff and how they
> \>> interact with our customers by e-mail. I am
> \>> willing to address the issue but wonder if a
> \>> formal policy should be issued by someone
> \>> higher up.

> \>>> Last week I heard from one of our regular
> \>>> customers about an inappropriate e-mail he
> \>>> received from a service rep he has been
> \>>> working with for several years. I guess the
> \>>> rep presumed they were friends and felt
> \>>> comfortable sharing the material with the
> \>>> customer. We should take action. But what
> \>>> action and who should take it?

In some cases, primarily with the use of formatted e-mail, the replies get indented and older replies are reduced in type size. Such messages can be incredibly difficult to read:

> I agree with what you're saying, and believe
> we can work together to resolve the issue.
> I too have a few concerns about who should
> take the lead on this one. Let's kick it up the
> ladder and see what Tom thinks.

>> This is something that needs to be resolved
>> quickly if we are going to avoid serious
>> issues down the road with our staff and how
>> they interact with our customers by e-mail. I
>> am willing to address the issue but wonder if
>> a formal policy should be issued by someone
>> higher up.

>>> Last week I heard from one of our
>>> regular customers about an inappropriate
>>> e-mail he received from a service rep he has
>>> been working with for several years. I guess
>>> the rep presumed they were friends and felt
>>> comfortable sharing the material with the
>>> customer. We should take action. But what
>>> action and who should take it?

I'm sure you've seen even more convoluted e-mail messages. In short, you are better off reading the message, clicking reply and replying in full, just as if you were composing an original message.

Changing the subject line

E-mail messages can fly back and forth at breakneck speed. Often two people start communicating about one topic and, as the e-mail moves back and forth, they cover other topics.

If the subject of your e-mail message changes after a couple of replies, change the subject line to reflect the change of topic. This will make it easier for you to file and track down e-mail messages related to particular topics. You can keep the old subject line in brackets as you change subject lines to let the reader know you are continuing an old discussion but addressing a new topic.

Original e-mail subject:

How to write e-mail messages

As you write, the topic of your e-mail message changes to how to reply to e-mail messages, so change the topic:

Replying to e-mail (Was: How to write e-mail messages)

Auto-Reply

E-mail seems to be all-pervasive. Mobile e-mail devices, such as the BlackBerry, the iPhone, and other smart phones, mean many people can never get away from it. There may be times when you need to take some downtime from e-mail. And there may be times when you simply cannot access your e-mail. If you are in a meeting or otherwise out of the office, if you are on vacation, or if you want some time away from e-mail, use auto-reply (if your e-mail system allows you to do so) to let senders know that your reply will be delayed. You might even be able to use auto-reply to answer the types of questions you normally get or to provide the kind of information you frequently provide.

When you use auto-reply, senders get an automatically generated message that informs them that you are out of the office. Most auto-reply systems let you compose the e-mail message that senders will receive. Take some time to think about who might be e-mailing you and what they might need—especially if you are dealing with customers or other people who are not part of your organization. In your auto-reply message

- acknowledge receipt of the e-mail;
- let the sender know when you will be back in the office or otherwise able to reply;
- if you have a back up, include that person's name, e-mail address, and phone number.

However, you might want to go beyond the basics in your auto-reply message. You might want to cover a few other work-related points. Keep your reply simple, but make sure it is detailed enough so people who e-mail you with important or urgent requests know what their options are. For instance, you might want to add a short FAQ (answers to frequently asked questions) to your standard auto-reply message (although you do not need to use the FAQ question and answer format). Your reply might include lines as simple as these:

- If you need information about <subject>, please contact <name, contact information>.
- If you are concerned about delivery of <item>, please contact <name, contact information>.

- If this is a customer service issue, please contact <name, contact information>.

Of course, depending on the nature of your typical e-mail communication, your auto-reply can include much more information. Whatever you include, you want your readers to understand that they are receiving an auto-reply and you want them to know what their options are. In short, you still want your reply to be as clear, concise, and focused as possible.

Note: if you have subscribed to any e-mail mailing lists, you should unsubscribe from them before using the auto-reply function so that out of the office replies are not sent to the list every time you receive a message from the list.

To, Cc, and Bcc

When you send e-mail to someone, you enter the person's e-mail address into the To field. If you want to send an e-mail message to several people, you can enter all their e-mail addresses into the To field. However, if there is a primary person and secondary contact, you are better off entering the e-mail address of the primary contact in the To field and entering the e-mail addresses of the secondary contacts in the Cc (carbon copy) field.

The primary contact is usually a person (or persons) who must reply or take action. Those who receive the e-mail message as a Cc, often receive it as an FYI (for your information). However, they might have to take some action based on the content of the e-mail message. Make sure you are clear about who should do what.

Think twice about using Cc in an e-mail message to a large group of people. If someone receives an e-mail message as a Cc and hits reply-to-all, the reply goes to all the people who received the original e-mail message. That is not a problem, unless you do not want all the people on the list to receive replies. If you are working with people who are new to e-mail or do not understand the reply and reply-to-all functions, you might want to let them know how to reply.

In addition, when you Cc a group of people, you expose the all the e-mail addresses of the people who received your message. Again, that is not a problem if the group does not mind. However, if you do not want to expose e-mail addresses, and/or if you do not want the people you have e-mailed to receive replies, use blind carbon copy (Bcc).

If you send an e-mail message to a primary contact and send it Bcc to others, the person in the To field cannot reply-to-all and will not be able to see the names and e-mail addresses of those you sent the message to Bcc.

Bcc is often used when you are engaged in a sticky situation or one that political and you want to copy someone without letting the primary contact know that you have sent the e-mail message to another or to others. However, you can use Bcc and let the person in the To field know that you have sent the e-mail message to other recipients using Bcc.

To format or not to format?

There was, for a while, a big debate over the use of formatted and plain text e-mail. If you send an e-mail in plain text, you cannot control the font (also known as typeface) or text size or color. Formatted e-mail messages, on the other hand, let you:

- Use different typestyles and different fonts, such as Times, Arial, or Broadway; however, I suggest you avoid fancy, difficult-to-read fonts.

- Use different type sizes. I suggest you stick with one type size, unless you are actually sending a report by e-mail and want to use a larger type size for a title and subheads. However, I suggest you use Word or Acrobat (PDF files) for reports.

- Use different colors, bold, italic, and underline; you may want to use a second color to emphasize a particular point, but I suggest you use a second color (as well as bold, italic, and underline) sparingly or your formatting will interfere with the clarity of your communication.

- Embed images, graphics, icons, or smileys ☺. I suggest you do not use smileys and that you keep the embedding of images or graphics to a minimum. Again, use Word or PDFs if you have to send a message with images, charts, or graphics.

In short, if you use formatted e-mail, use black type (one font, one size) on a white background, with no or few images. Use bold judiciously on subheads in a longer e-mail message and you can use bullets and numbering if you want to convey a list of facts or ideas. Beyond that, keep your formatting simple and don't use smileys. Let your message and tone clearly communicate what you are saying. In addition, keep in mind that your e-mail message might be forwarded to other recipients. Ask yourself how you would feel if someone you did not know received a message full of smileys that you originated.

Hi... Dear... Regards... Cheers

People often ask me if they should start their e-mail messages with one of the following greetings:

> Hi,
> Hi <first name>,
> Dear <first name>,
> Dear Mr./Ms. <last name>:

E-mail messages are less formal than letters. If you are writing a letter and you don't know the person you are writing, you would start it like this:

> Dear Mr. Smith:

If you know the person, you can start it like this:

> Dear Chris,

If you are e-mailing someone you don't know for the first time, and if the person is a superior, prospect, or customer, you can start it like this:

> Dear Mr. Smith:

However, if you know the person or have a sense of who the person is, you can start your e-mail message like this:

> Hi <first name>,
> Dear <first name>,

If you are not sure what to do, answering the following questions should help you decide:

- How well do you know the person?

- How formal or informal is the message?
- Is this a quick reminder or is it similar to a business letter?
- If you have no salutation, how will the reader feel?
- How has the reader addressed you previously?

If in doubt, use "Hi" or whatever opening you are comfortable with. In fact, for internal e-mail to someone you write frequently, and even for e-mail sent to people outside your company or organization, you might want to simply start with your opening paragraph. After all, the recipient sees who the message is from and the subject line, so in some way, you have already dispensed with the pleasantries. Or you might want to use "Hi" for your first message of the day, but skip the salutations for all replies.

If you are replying to an e-mail message, you can simply parrot what the sender has done. On the other hand, if the sender has been very formal and you want to bring a modest degree of informality to the communication, you can start the message by saying "Hi" or "Hi <first name>". (If your organization has a formal policy on how you should begin e-mail messages, especially when writing customers or suppliers, simply follow the policy.)

People are sometimes unsure of how to end e-mail messages. They want to know if they should end e-mail with

> Regards,
> Sincerely,
> Cheers,

They also want to know if they should use their first name or first and last name. Again, you can follow the lead of the sender when you are replying. You can also ask yourself the questions listed above and let your answers guide you. At the same time, it's hard to go wrong with something like this:

> Regards,
> Paul Lima

But you can go wrong with the above closing if that is all you use. Ask yourself what information you would like to see in an e-mail signature. I suspect you wouldn't mind seeing the person's name, title or position, and company, as well as an e-mail address, phone number, and website address.

With that in mind, compose a signature file (Outlook and most other e-mail applications let you do this), and set up your e-mail application to insert your e-mail signature automatically at the end of each message. Here is my standard signature:

> Regards,
> Paul Lima
> Freelance writer/writing trainer
> www.paullima.com
> writer@paullima.com
> 416-628-6005

Notice the e-mail address and phone number in my signature. These days you never know where people are when they receive your e-mail messages. You don't know what contact information they have on you. You don't know if they are going to print or forward your message. So it doesn't hurt to supply them with your most important contact information. If I worked for a company, I would also include my title and the company name.

At the same time, if your company has a signature policy (it often includes a disclaimer about the e-mail message being a private communication), then use the corporate signature.

Many companies want all employees to use a disclaimer like this:

> This communication is intended for use by the individual(s) to whom it is specifically addressed and should not be read by, or delivered to, any other person. Such communication may contain privileged or confidential information. If you have received this communication in error, please notify the sender and permanently delete the communication. Thank you for your cooperation.

I find such disclaimers overkill. However, if your company has a signature and/or a disclaimer policy, then you need to follow it. E-mail messages are official company communications and can be referred to in case of legal action or other disputes. So follow company protocol when sending, and replying to, e-mail.

Chapter 14: Media Releases

Most business writers do not write media releases. They tend to be produced by the public relations or communication departments of most organizations, or contracted out to a public relations company. In addition, I cannot tell you everything you need to know about writing and issuing media releases and media advisories in one chapter. (There is much more about this topic in my book, *How to Write Media Releases to Promote Your Business, Organization or Event.*) Nevertheless, I wanted to include a chapter on writing media releases here because well-written media releases are exceptionally focused documents.

If you had any doubts about the importance of knowing your W5 (who, what, where, when, and why) before you write, I hope seeing the media releases presented in this chapter will help dispel those doubts. In addition, if you had any doubts about getting organized before you write, I hope you will see how outlining your W5 helps you write powerful openings that capture the attention of a well-defined audience.

Finally, you will see how the major or most important W5 elements are used in the headline, subhead, opening paragraph, and quote paragraph of a media release.

Doing that is like using the most important thing you have to say in a subject line and opening paragraph and confirming it in your closing. In addition, when we start writing longer documents, such as proposals and reports, you will see some repetition parallels—particularly in how you present your important information in the title of your longer document, as well as in your executive summary, introduction, and conclusion.

In short, a modicum of repetition is your friend when it comes to business writing. If you have something important to say, say it several times. That is not being redundant. That is placing emphasis where it should be placed. This is something that well-written media releases do effectively, and all business writing should do.

But before we look at how media releases do it, let's define a media release.

What is a media release?

A media release is a formal one- or two-page document that tells a newsworthy story to the media.

If your story is of interest, the release may appear as written, either in whole or in part. If your story is seen as particularly newsworthy, an editor or reporter may call you to set up an interview for more information.

If the editor feels your release is not newsworthy, or if she has no space for it, then your release will not be used. You have no control over this. However, if you target a concise, well-written, informative release at the right editors at the appropriate media outlets, you improve the chance of having your release used or having a reporter call you to set up an interview before writing an article based on the release. (So if you send out a release, you must be prepared to speak to the media.)

Why bother with media relations?

Consumers regard advertising with a degree of skepticism. Yet, if they read the same message in a newspaper or magazine article (or here it during a news program on television or on the radio), they are be more inclined to believe it or seek out further information. This can have a positive impact on your bottom line or on your social or political cause. In addition, media relations offer a cost-effective way for organizations to get their messages out to their community and stakeholders. Media releases do not replace marketing and advertising; however, they should be used in conjunction with marketing and advertising plans.

Sample media release

Before we go any further, let's look at a sample media release.

WIDGET CO. PRODUCES 1 MILLION WIDGETS IN 5 YEARS

Production Achievement Surpasses Expectations, Maintains Focus on Quality: One Millionth Widget Rolls Off Line August 1

Brampton, Ontario July 28, 2010 – Widget Co. Inc. today announced that its one-millionth Widget will roll off the assembly line on August 1, 2010, at its production facility in Brampton, Ontario. Widget Co. experienced exponential growth, exceeding industry expectations, to reach this remarkable milestone in five short years.

"We are extremely proud of our employees, the people who put quality into every Widget produced by Widget Co. They are the people who enabled Widget Co. to produce our one-millionth Widget in five years, growing from a production run of under 25,000 Widgets in year one to over 350,000 this year," says Tom Kohl, CEO and Founder of Widget Co. Inc. "While our growth has been remarkable, we never waivered from our commitment to quality and innovation," Mr. Kohl added.

Widget Co.'s real time online customization and ordering process, its innovative ISO 9000-certified continuous improvement production techniques, and its just-in-time delivery methods have allowed the company to grow in a planned, cost-effective manner while delivering quality products to Mega-Widget manufacturers across Canada and the United States.

The Widget Production Association of Canada (WPAC), at its Annual General Conference held last month in Toronto, lauded Widget Co. for its impressive and unprecedented growth in Widget production. "Widget Co. has contributed to the growth of this industry as a whole, while focusing on quality," said WPAC president, Sarah Wise.

- ### -

About Widget Co. Inc.: Founded in 2005, privately held, ISO 9000-certified Widget Co. Inc. produces high-quality Widgets used in the manufacturing of Mega-Widgets at manufacturing plants across North America. Widget Co. employs 57 engineers, production workers, and sales and administrative staff at its Brampton, Ontario, production facility.

For More Information: Mary Press: 905-555-1212 or mp@widgetco.com

W5 in the media release

Let's deconstruct the media release so we can review W5 components used in the release:

Who: Widget Co.

What: Produces 1 million widgets

Where: At its plant in Brampton, Ontario

When: In five years; August 1

Why: There are often multiple "whys" in this media release (and most other communication).

What are the "whys" here? There is "why announce this?" The company is hoping for exposure in newspapers and magazines that potential clients read, but can't say that. Then there is "why is this news?" Other companies may have produced a million widgets, but no one has done it faster. The media loves records. You need to be clear on your whys before you can determine your why priorities, including which whys you will and which whys you will not address.

The W5 is the foundation of media releases, even though there are often other components you have to add to releases (or any other document). For instance, notice the emphasis on quality. It could be there to assure possible customers that widgets can be mass produced while maintaining quality. So think beyond the W5 for other aspects you have to address, and weave them into your release in a clear, concise, coherent narrative.

Media release components

Let's take a closer look at the components of the media release. Notice, as well, how the major aspects of the who, what, where, when, and/or why elements are repeated in the headline, subhead line, opening paragraph, and quote paragraph.

Headline: WIDGET CO. PRODUCES 1 MILLION WIDGETS IN 5 YEARS

Subhead: Production Achievement Surpasses Expectations While Maintaining Focus on Quality: One Millionth Widget Rolls Off Line August 1

Dateline: Brampton, Ontario July 28, 2010

Opening paragraph: Widget Co. Inc. today announced that its one-millionth Widget will roll off the assembly line on August 1, 2010, at its production facility in Brampton, Ontario. Widget Co. experienced exponential growth, exceeding industry expectations, to reach this remarkable milestone in five short years.

Quote paragraph: "We are extremely proud of our employees, the people who put quality into every Widget produced by Widget Co. They are the people who enabled Widget Co. to produce our one-millionth Widget in five years, growing from a production run of under 25,000 Widgets in year one to over 350,000 this year," says Tom Kohl, CEO and Founder of Widget Co. Inc. "While our growth has been remarkable, we never waivered from our commitment to quality and innovation," Mr. Kohl added.

Support paragraphs: A series of, background paragraphs followed by hash marks (###) that indicate the end of the portion of the release you hope will be published.

About paragraph: About Widget Co. Inc....

Contact information: For More Information: Mary Press: 905-555-1212 or mp@widgetco.com

Focus is key

As with any writing, an effective media release should focus on one aspect of business—something newsworthy that will turn the crank of an editor or reporter. You should also focus your media contacts. In other words, don't send your business news media release to the food editor (unless you are a food company). Don't send your theater production announcement to sports reporters (unless your play is sports related). Don't send your enterprise software announcement to magazines for women like *Chatelaine* or *Ms.* (unless it will allow companies to address issues related to women).

In short, you should have a clear idea of what you want to say (message focus), to whom you want to say it (target audience), and which media outlets will reach your target audience. Then you should write what you have to say, following the standard media release format presented here. Doing all of that will increase your chance of a hit—having your release picked up and used by media outlets.

The key to writing an effective media release lies in understanding and articulating your W5—who, what, where, when, and why. The most important aspects of your W5 appear in your headline, subhead-line, lead or opening paragraph, and quote paragraph.

Note: Writers of media releases don't take the time to interview subjects hoping for a solid, focused quote. Rather, it is the norm for the writer to make up the quote and then ask the spokesperson to review it, revise it as may be required, based on corporate policies and priorities, and approve it.

In addition to the judicious repetition of the W5, notice the repetition of keywords, such as "quality," in the Widget release. As a writer—and this applies to anything you write—you need to know what you want to stress and you need to stress it by weaving it into your writing in an unobtrusive manner while making sense based on the content and context of your message. In the Widget release, the news is the production achievement; however, the company needs its target market to know that this was done without compromising quality.

A closer look at leads

To capture the attention of the editor or journalist who receives your media release, the headline and subhead line should contain the most important W5 aspects; the lead or opening paragraph or two should contain the entire W5. With that in mind, here are several sample leads, followed by one more media release and a writing exercise. See if you can identify the W5 in each.

> Montreal, June 18, 2001 – West Jet announced today that it is extending its special first anniversary sale of one-way, $1 fares from Toronto to all of its Canadian destinations. A return flight at regular, low summer rates must also be purchased. Regular taxes and surcharges are extra.

◼ ◼ ◼

> Toronto, Ontario, Aug. 24, 2004 – Working Women Community Centre today announces that it was selected as the first Ontario site for Home Instruction for Parents of Preschool Youngsters, a school readiness program developed in Israel to maximize, through early intervention, the educational potential of young children in low-income families.

◼ ◼ ◼

Toronto, Ontario, January 4, 2009 — Paul Lima, a successful freelance writer, author, and writing trainer, today announced the release of his tenth book, *How to Write A Non-fiction Book in 60 Days*. Available as a PDF file or trade paperback (www.paullima.com/books), *How to Write A Non-fiction Book in 60 Days* helps consultants, workshop leaders and others who aspire to write non-fiction books overcome the number one barrier to success—the lack of a planned approached to organizing and writing their books.

◼ ◼ ◼

The following is one of my favorite leads because it packs so much information into one sentence. At first, it may seem convoluted, but if you read it slowly, it makes sense:

Montreal, Sept. 20, 1998 – The Honorable Claude Drouin, Secretary of State (Economic Development Agency of Canada for the Regions of Quebec) and MP for Beauce, on behalf of the Honorable Jane Stewart, Minister of Human Resources Development Canada (HRDC), will participate in a commemorative tree-planting ceremony at the Commission scolaire de la Beauce-Etchemin of Saint-Georges, to commemorates 75 years of public pensions in Canada.

Note: I said this is one of my favorites, but for all the wrong reasons. It shows you how to pack one heck of a lot of information into one sentence. It is, however a long and convoluted sentence. It was written for the internal approval of political masters and not to excite the media.

Please do not write opening sentences like it if you want journalists to read your media releases (and do not write openings like this for any other document, if you want it to be read. Again, the sentence packs a lot in, and it makes grammatical sense, but that does not mean it is clear or concise.

Sample media release

Here is another sample media release for your perusal:

Youth Volunteer Association Puts Time on Charities' Side

Young People Bid Volunteer Time for Art and Support Charities on August 1 at YVA Silent Auction in Toronto

Toronto, Ontario July 15, 2009 – In a twist on the standard silent auction, young people can bid time in exchange for original art and help three local charities in need of volunteers at a Youth Volunteer Association (YVA) silent auction to be held in the lobby of the CBC building on August 1 from 7:00 PM to 10:00 PM.

Instead of bidding money, silent auction participants will bid time, in two-hour increments, for over 100 pieces of original art donated to the YVA silent auction by Canadian artists. The winning bidders will then donate their time to any one of three participating charities—the United Way, Canadian Cancer Society, and Salvation Army.

"Young people are often strapped for cash and charities are often strapped for volunteers. So this is a perfect match," said Jim James, YVA founder. "By encouraging youth to give their time to charities, we are letting them know they can contribute and make a difference, without reaching for their wallets. We are also fostering an important spirit of volunteerism."

Combined, the United Way, Canadian Cancer Society, and Salvation Army use over 5,000 volunteers contributing almost 500 million hours per year to a vast variety of activities that would not get done if it were not for volunteers.

"Driving cancer patients to and from chemotherapy appointments takes time, and if it were not for volunteer drivers, many cancer patients would have to rely on taxis or public transit. But too often they cannot afford cabs and they are too weak to take transit," said Mary Heart, president of the Canadian Cancer Society. "Volunteers are essential."

"We are pleased to participate in the YVA silent auction," she added. "It is an innovative way to boost volunteerism and to encourage young people to get involved with charitable organizations."

The doors to the silent auction open at 6:30 P.M. Many of the contributing artists will be creating art during the event and popular indie bands Funk-a-delic and sPunk will perform. Admittance is free, but people are encouraged to bring canned goods and other non-perishable items for the Toronto Food Bank.

- ### -

About Youth Volunteer Association: Founded in 2000, the YVA (www.yva.com) is an independent, nonprofit organization dedicated to encouraging volunteerism among people under 30. Over 10,000 YVA volunteers across Canada have logged almost one million volunteer hours since YVA's inception.

For More Information: Contact: Jean Roi: 905-555-1212 or jroi@yva.com

Your turn to write

Now it is your turn to write. Review the two case studies on the next couple of pages and then follow these instructions:

- Pick one of the case studies.
- Refine the idea suggested to promote the event. (To what extent you refine the idea I will leave up to you. The goal is to write a clear, focused media release that appropriately reflects the company or organization and meets the stated purpose.)
- Outline your W5 before you write.
- Write your lead—literally the first paragraph or two of your release.
- Write your headline and subhead line based on your release.
- Add a quote paragraph.
- Write two or three other paragraphs to fill in any other pertinent details (make up any facts you might need to flush out the release).
- Include an "about" paragraph and contact information (as you see with the sample releases in this session).

Case Study A

The Canadian Apple Growers Association (CAGA) has hired your public relations agency to stage and promote an event in New York City. The purpose is to attract media attention to create public awareness of the Ambrosia apple.

The CAGA's goal is to boost sales of Canadian apples in the United States. Since the Ambrosia apple is not grown in the United States, CAGA feels this apple offers a unique marketing opportunity.

Background information: The Ambrosia apple is a chance seedling discovered in the early 1980s in B.C.; it's now grown in B.C. and Ontario. It's a good-quality red apple that ripens in late fall. Its parents are Golden Delicious and Starking Delicious.

The fruit is medium to large in size with an attractive red blush and faint stripes on a cream or yellow background; crisp; sweet; low acid; very juicy; distinct, pleasant aroma; mild flavor. It's excellent eaten fresh or for fresh salads as the flesh is slow to oxidize (brown).

There is an Internet rumor that the apple has been used as an aphrodisiac.

The idea: To hold a fall fair Canadian-style in the Big Apple. The fair would run the first Saturday and Sunday in October in Central Park. It would include hay-rides, pony rides, an apple pie baking contest, an apple pie eating competition, free apple cider, and balloons, and, of course, free Ambrosia apples.

There would be music playing all day—fiddling and jug bands as well as folk music—and square-dances, including free square-dance lessons.

Your task: If you choose to work on this case, refine the event as you see fit. Outline your W5 and write a release that will capture the attention and hold the interest of the media and, through the media, your target market.

When reading the case study, think about what you should leave in and what you should leave out of your media release. The release will be sent to food and lifestyle editors and journalists as well as reporters who cover community events. The CAGA spokesperson that you will quote in the release is Johnny McDonald, president of CAGA.

Case Study B

Henri Blanc has hired your public relations agency to promote an event in Toronto to attract media attention and to create awareness about his new upscale French bistro in Yorkville, Chez Restaurant.

Background information: There are more restaurants per capita in the City of Toronto than in almost any other city in North America; competition among high-end restaurants is fierce. Chez Restaurant has a prime location, valet parking, and a cordon bleu chef, M. Boeuf. He was trained in Paris, France, where he worked for twenty years in five-star restaurants.

Your menu is world class, as is your décor. Your prices reflect your chef, menu, and the dining experience, which is private, personal, and exquisite. You expect to attract celebrities, CEOs, and deal-makers.

The idea: To invite selected media—business editors and restaurant reviewers—to a grand opening gala party featuring fine finger foods and wine tasting. Jazz singer and crooner Michael Barns would provide the entertainment. The event would include brief presentations by M. Blanc and M. Boeuf. The gala will be held the day before the opening of the Toronto International Film Festival; a number of movie stars, producers, and directors have accepted invitations to the opening.

The invited media and guests will receive private invitations. This release announces the grand opening gala, complete with red carpet. The goal is to create buzz with a big splash outside the restaurant—fans and media lining the red carpet; lots of red carpet photo opportunities—while providing guests with an intimate and private experience inside the restaurant.

Your task: Outline your W5 and write a release that will capture the attention and hold the interest of the media and your target market.

> **Write a media release or an opening paragraph and headline/subhead for either case study before you continue to read.**

Chapter 15: Persuasive Writing

If your purpose, when you write, is to motivate somebody to do something or to think a particular way about something, then you have to make your purpose clear and write persuasively. Of course, before you can persuade people to do anything—such as buy something—you have to capture their attention, hold their interest, and reinforce or adjust their attitude. Only then can you motivate them to act.

It would be grand if, to capture a reader's attention, we could just do like advertisers do and use words such as *free, new and improved, introducing*, or *announcing*. In some ways, we can. These are trigger words—words that capture the attention of consumers and motivate them to read on, at least until they determine whether they are interested in whatever is being advertised. To capture the attention of your audience, you have to know who your audience is (part of the writing process), determine what their trigger words are, and use them effectively—in titles of reports, openings of letters, subject lines of e-mail messages, and so on.

I know it's all easier said than done; however, if writing were easy, then you wouldn't be reading this book.

Persuasive writing is not just about getting someone to buy something—to spend money on a purchase. Any time you want people to do something—take any action—you are trying to persuade them or get them to "buy in" even though you may not be trying to get them to buy.

As with all business writing, persuasive writing must be focused and must avoid ambiguity if it is to convince readers to adopt the writer's point of view. In short, persuasive writing tries to

- educate the reader about an issue,
- reinforce ideas the reader has, or
- convince the reader to change his or her point of view.

Persuasive writing primarily uses facts and figures and appeals to logic to persuade someone to do something, but politicians, social activists, and charities may also salt their persuasive writing with emotional appeals. Although business writing should avoid playing on emotion, effective business writing has to influences the attitude of the readers. Sometimes, this involves an emotional shift within the reader.

Who persuades whom?

Proposals and reports often use persuasive writing to convince readers to take defined actions. For instance, a union might produce a report to lobby the government to change employment safety legislation, to pass new legislation that forces companies to meet new safety standards, or to spend money on training or unemployment compensation. Marketing departments often write internal proposals to lobby for the introduction of a new product or service or for the expenditure of money on new marketing campaigns. IT departments often write proposals that justify—using return on investment (ROI) and/or increased productivity—the expenditure of money on new IT systems.

Advertising agencies and public relations firms must persuade potential clients to pick them to advertise or promote products, services, or events. It's not enough to say, "Based on our reputation and experience, you should trust and hire us." Reputation and experience are important. However, the agency also has to demonstrate its creative insight and show how they would promote the prospective client's product. This requires a proposal that convinces the prospective client that the agency or firm

- understands the "product" in relation to the intended target market,
- has the creative means to communicate the promotional message to the intended target market,
- can deliver the campaign within an agreed upon budget.

In other words, it is the agency's job to link the proposed advertising campaign or media relations event to the client's product/service and the intended market.

AIAA revisited

As I have mentioned before, to be effective, writing must do the following:

- capture *Attention*
- maintain *Interest*
- change or reinforce *Attitude*
- motivate *Action*

The title of a proposal and its executive summary must capture the reader's attention. To do that, it must use language—words, phrases, and sentences—that appeal to and engage the reader. Trigger words, in other words.

Then the proposal must maintain interest. Think of your reader asking questions such as these: "What is this about? Why should I read it? Why is this important? What is the situation now? How will it change? Why should it change? Can we afford to do it? Can we afford not to do it?" If you can answer those questions, you will hold the interest of your readers.

Of course, the proposal must influence attitude. Think of your reader asking: "What's in it for me?" or "What's in it for my organization, department, customers?" If you can answer those questions while building trust and overcoming possible objections, then you will influence, change, or reinforce attitude. Persuasive writing should also acknowledge (and refute) conflicting opinions or opposing points of view. This helps make a proposal appear objective and helps build credibility.

Finally, you need to motivate action. To do so, you need to know what you want the reader to do and then you have to ask the reader to do it. In addition, you have to tell the reader how to do it—call this toll free number, visit this website, mail your member of Parliament, implement these five recommendations, build the highway in this location not that location, buy here, buy now, and so on.

What's in it for me?

Review the following scenarios and determine your answer to "What's in it for me?" You don't have to write a formal document. Simply list the points you would address and note why you would address them. To start, clarify your purpose and the action you want the reader to take.

Also, think about what's in it for the reader. Think of the benefits for the reader and the consequences (if the reader fails to act), as well as any objections the reader might have. List all benefits, consequences, and objections. Before you write a proposal you will, of course, have to decide if you should include any or all of the benefits and any or all of the consequences or try to overcome any or all objections in your final document. However, you want that to be a conscious decision. With that in mind, jot down all the points you can think of first. Then, when you outline a proposal, you would indicate which ones you would include in your final document.

In addition, think about the tone you want to strike in each message. Keep in mind who you are and who you are writing in each scenario. That has an impact on your purpose, tone, and content.

If it helps, use this format to help you organize your thoughts:

- Purpose:
- Benefits:
- Consequences:
- Objections:
- Action:
- Tone:

This exercise will help you develop the habit of answering the "What's in it for me?" question (from the reader's point of view) before you write. It also helps with the creation of outlines, another *before you write* activity.

Scenarios

Scenario 1: Labor Organizer

You are a labor organizer trying to unionize a Floor-Mart store. Floor-Mart is notorious for combating union activity. It pays wages that are slightly below industry standards and hires more part-time workers (rather than full-time workers) to save on benefits and overtime. You are writing a letter that will go to the home of each Floor-Mart employee at the store you are trying to organize. You have chatted with several employees and it is generally understood that there will be an attempt to organize a union. However, this letter will be your first formal contact with all employees. You want them to show up at a meeting in a week's time so you can state your case.

◩   ◩   ◩

Scenario 2: Floor-Mart Executive

You are a Floor-Mart executive. A labor organizer is trying to unionize employees at a Floor-Mart store. Your company prefers not to have unions, as unions work to negotiate higher wages and benefits. Floor-Mart has cut costs to be as competitive as possible in a competitive retail environment. You understand that the union organizers have held several meetings, and you want to state the company's concerns. You have to walk a fine line as you do not want the union organizers to accuse the company of using scare tactics to engage in union busting. You need to make employees aware of the negative consequences of unionizing without threatening them. You are doing this in a letter that is going out to all employees with their next paycheck.

◩   ◩   ◩

Scenario 3: Communication Designer

You are an employee in a small company that produces widgets. Your job is to design promotional brochures and product sheets, and to maintain the company website. You are doing this on a PC but would prefer to do it on a Mac because of the design applications to which you would have access. The owner is concerned because Macs cost more and because nobody in the office will be able to use the Mac for rush jobs that might occur when you are on vacation. Macs, however, can now run in Windows mode. In addition, Microsoft has announced a new operating system, which means your present computer will soon need to be upgraded. Since the company is going to have to spend money on a new computer, you want the business owner to spend it on a Mac. You believe you can produce better quality brochures and website pages in less time on the Mac. Write a short proposal to the company owner.

◩   ◩   ◩

Scenario 4: Health and Safety Trainer

You are the chairperson of the company health and safety committee. The provincial government has just introduced new hazardous waste handling materials safety standards (HWHMSS). Training in HWHMSS is mandatory. Training for administrative staff who are not likely to handle hazardous waste lasts one hour. You cannot put more than ten people in a class. You had three months to conduct training for 120 administrative staff members. Although all staff members signed up for training, most of them did not show up for the scheduled training sessions. You have one month left and seventy-five employees to train. If you do not complete the training, the company could face fines or even be shut down. While the government will likely extend the training period for one month, the company's liability insurance policy might be in jeopardy if all staff are not trained within the next month. Write the memo that motivates staff to sign up and attend the next round of training sessions.

> Use the pre-writing *purpose, benefits, consequences, objections, action, tone* format to determine *what's in it for the reader*, before you read on.

So, what's in it for me?

Review the lists below, but don't worry if your lists are not the same as the ones presented here. You may have interpreted the cases differently, depending on your background, education, and work experience. Do, however, compare your lists with the ones below. You may see some points that you should have made; you may also see that you have some perfectly valid points that do not appear in these lists.

The main point of this exercise is to demonstrate the importance of thinking before you write so that you will write effective, persuasive documents. I also hope this exercise also demonstrates the importance of jotting down the points you want to make before you begin to write. In other words, why try to hold all of this in your head as you write, when you can jot down the information before you write. Doing so means you will be less likely to leave out any important points or, to put it more persuasively, you will be more likely to cover all the important points you need to make.

Scenario 1: Labor Organizer

Purpose: To Invite Floor-Mart employees at a particular store to attend a union organizing meeting.

Benefits: The union will bargain for higher wages, more full-time positions, better benefits.

Consequences: Continue low wages, part-time hours, and poor or no benefits; union dues if union is accepted; possible strike.

Objections: Floor-Mart might react negatively and cut jobs or close the store if the company discovers employees are organizing a union.

Action: Show up for the meeting; do not ask them to respond as they might find it intimidating to do so.

Tone: Don't be strident; that might scare off the undecided; focus on benefits, not consequences.

◼   ◼   ◼

Scenario 2: Floor-Mart Executive

Purpose: To inform Floor-Mart employees of the consequences of unionizing.

Benefits: By keeping wages reasonable, you can be competitive and survive. You can also hire more employees and provide better service, which leads to increased sales and the hiring of more employees.

Objections: Wages are low, benefits are non-existent; only a union can help. Shifts are granted in an arbitrary manner, with no respect to seniority.

Consequences: Fewer employees if wages go up. A strike if union demands are deemed excessive. Closing of the store if employees unionize.

Action: Read the letter and think about their choices.

Tone: Don't be strident; that might drive some employees to the union. Focus on benefits, not consequences; don't want to be perceived as threatening—not in a first letter to employees.

Note: Some states/provinces/countries have laws that restrict what an employer can say under such circumstances; don't say anything that can be perceived as breaking the law.

◼ ◼ ◼

Scenario 3: Communication Designer

Purpose: To persuade your employer to buy (or let you buy) a Mac.

Benefits: Produce a greater variety of promotional material, including print, Web pages, and even audio and video if required. Produce material faster; therefore able to meet tight deadlines. All employees can use the Mac running in Windows mode. Macs are far less susceptible to viruses and can be relied on if any PCs are infected. A small price premium gets a more versatile, more reliable system.

Consequences: Being a Mac lover, you can't think of any consequences to buying a Mac. (However, allow me to say it will cost more; software for it is more expensive; running in Windows mode makes it susceptible to viruses.)

Objections: Macs are expensive. Other employees can't use the Mac. Company will require PC and Mac tech support.

Action: Purchase a Mac instead of a PC when it's time to upgrade.

Tone: Positive and objective. You achieve objectivity by acknowledging the additional cost. However, play up the versatility (better material produced faster), reliability, and compatibility.

◼ ◼ ◼

Scenario 4: Health and Safety Trainer

Purpose: To motivate employees to take HWHMSS training.

Benefits: People will know how to handle hazardous material should they encounter it.

Consequences: Mandatory training. The company could be fined if all staff members are not trained. Insurance can be withdrawn if all staff are not trained. Fines and a lack of insurance could mean the end of the company, and the end of jobs.

Objections: We won't use the training; we don't need it. We are too busy to take the training.

Action: Sign up for, and take, the next available training session.

Tone: Take a strong position: play up the consequences—to the company and potentially to employees. If company policy allows it, let employees know that without the training they will be suspended so the company is not fined or shut down.

Note: Administrative staff has resisted training because, in their minds, they do not need it. Even though they will probably never use the training, it is mandatory. As you have tried, and failed, to get all staff to take the training, you can use a strong tone. If this was your first memo to administrative staff, on the other hand, you'd want to use a lighter, yet encouraging, tone.

Chapter 16: Sales Letters

As the name implies, sales letters are used to sell something to someone. In order to sell anyone anything, you have to persuade him or her to take action—to buy. However, if you are selling an expensive (and possibly complex) product or service—an IT solution, a backhoe for commercial construction use, accounting and auditing services—the action you desire might not be "buy" even though you are writing a sales letter because people don't purchase expensive and complex products off the shelf the way they buy DVDs, books, or socks.

You might, instead, want the reader to take a pre-purchase action—call for more information, visit your website, arrange for a sales representative to call, and so on. In short, before you write a sales letter or any copy meant to persuade, you need to know what action you are trying to persuade the reader to take. If you don't know your purpose and the action you want to reader to take, how can you achieve your purpose and motivate the reader to take a particular action?

Knowing what you want the reader to do, and motivating the reader to do it, is at the heart of any persuasive message, such as sales letters, proposal cover letters, advertising copy, and direct response marketing copy. As I have said previously, however, anytime you want anyone to do something—even attend a meeting—you are "selling" and you have to motivate the person to act or respond (buy into what you want, so to speak). For this chapter, though, we will concentrate on writing sales letters and proposal cover letters.

The typical sales letter does the following:

- Lets the reader know your purpose—why you are writing
- Introduces you to the reader and makes a connection between you (your company, your products and/or your services, or your proposal) and the reader's problem, issue, or opportunity

- Demonstrates that you understand the client's objectives and, depending on the circumstance, the client's target market and how what you are selling or proposing relates to the client's objectives and/or target market
- Extols the virtues of your company, products and/or services or summarizes (and extols the virtues of) your proposal
- Calls for a defined action; motivates the reader to act

Three-section sales letter

Sales letters and proposal cover letters should be divided into three sections:

Introduction

- Hooks the reader (captures attention) with a line that relates to a problem, issue, opportunity, or situation that the reader is familiar with or can relate to
- Continues to hold the reader's interest by proposing a solution, alternative, or means of exploiting the opportunity
- Makes clear the purpose of the letter

Body

- Continues to hold interest; starts to influence attitude
- May overcome anticipated objections (major attitude adjustment technique)
- May include rationale for and/or benefits of proposal
- May include schedule (timelines) and a detailed projection of costs (proposed budget)

Conclusion

- Calls for action and outlines next steps and how to take them; details who proposes to do what for whom, when, where, and why
- May offer an incentive to motivate the reader to act
- Demonstrates willingness to answer questions or provide more details

You might use attention-grabbing subheadings that create distinct sections in a sales letter, but you do not have to. Either way, you should be aware that the role of each section, as described above, is distinct. Even so, you need to write so that there are logical transitions between sections and a logical flow from section to section.

Cold-call sales letter example

Let's look at a cold-call sales letter. Also known as an unsolicited sales letter or direct response marketing letter, a cold-call sales letter is a letter you send to someone who has not requested it. Some people call unsolicited letters "junk mail." Such letters might feel like junk mail to consumers who are bombarded with unsolicited credit card applications and sales flyers; however, cold-call sales letters are a staple of business-to-business communication. They are often used to make initial contact with a prospect or to generate leads for a company's sales force, as in the sales letter example below.

Note: If you send your sales letter by e-mail, and you do not have permission to e-mail a business or consumer, it will be considered spam and will most likely be deleted, no matter how legitimate your business is. Building e-mail lists and using permission-based e-mail marketing go beyond the scope of this book; however, if you are planning an e-mail marketing campaign, make sure you investigate how to properly build permission-based e-mail lists.

> Dear Ms. Bussman:
>
> Are you having trouble keeping your cool? When you turn on the air conditioning, do you feel as if you are wasting energy and money? PLR Air Conditioning would like to demonstrate how we can help you keep cool and save energy too—all for less than you might have imagined.
>
> We would like to demonstrate how the installation of a PLR air conditioning system will keep your plant and office cool and reduce energy costs. The demonstration takes 45 minutes, and it will not disrupt your business operations.
>
> We believe that you will find PLR systems to be practical, efficient, and economical.

PLR has been in the industrial heating and air conditioning business for over 40 years, servicing companies like yours. We are a member of the Better Business Bureau and have a stellar credit rating. You can view our client list and read a number of testimonials on our website, www.plr.com.

Please review the information in the enclosed brochure and call us for a demonstration. What do you have to lose? Certainly not your cool! To set up a demonstration, call 416-555-5555.

If you call us by May 31, we will conduct a free energy efficiency audit and show you 10 no-cost ways to cut your company's electricity bill.

Sincerely,
James P. Callahan
Sales Manager

Components of cold-call sales letter

Now, let's examine the component parts of the sales letter.

Introduction: The letter starts with humor (risky, I confess) to capture the attention of (hook) the reader. Notice how the word "cool" used in the introduction is related to the product, and how quickly the writer connects the opening line to the product—connects cool to air conditioning. By the third sentence, the reader knows exactly why the writer is writing (purpose)—to conduct a demonstration. Notice how the purpose is supported by a benefit statement implying cost savings. In other words, the writer is supporting his purpose by letting the reader know that PLR can solve a problem.

Are you having trouble keeping your cool? When you turn on the air conditioning, do you feel as if you are wasting energy and money? PLR Air Conditioning would like to demonstrate how we can help keep you cool and save energy too—all for less than you might have imagined.

Body: Once the purpose is established, the body expands on it while maintaining interest ands influencing attitude. The body overcomes a possible objection: *This will probably take all day.* No, it "takes 45 minutes." It also focuses on information that is of interest to the client by promising to "reduce the cost of energy," and to be "practical, efficient, economical."

> We would like to demonstrate how the installation of a PLR air conditioning system will keep your plant and office cool and reduce the cost of energy. The demonstration takes 45 minutes, and it will not disrupt your business operations.
>
> We believe that you will find PLR systems to be practical, efficient, and economical.

The company also uses the body to build trust, just in case the reader is wondering who the heck PLR is.

> PLR has been in business for over 40 years, servicing companies like yours. We are a member of the Better Business Bureau and have a stellar credit rating. You can view our client list and read a number of testimonials on our website, www.plr.com.

Conclusion: Here the letter asks the reader to do something—read a brochure and make a call. The writer would be happy if the reader just called, but if the reader is interested, but not quite convinced, she can review additional information in the brochure. The conclusion succinctly summarizes what the letter has been about and echoes the opening, as if reminding the reader what caught her attention in the first place—"What do you have to lose? Certainly not your cool!"

The conclusion also offers the reader a limited time incentive to act. Within ten days, PLR will know how effective its cold-call sales letter was. If the company sends out two hundred letters and has ten or twenty replies, the letter would be considered a direct mail success. With that in mind, if you are ever conducting a direct mail campaign, sample your audience first. Say you want to send out two thousand letters. Send out a hundred letters first and gauge the response. If you come up empty, you will want to review and revise your sales message.

Follow-up sales letter

In the post-demonstration follow-up sales letter, the same principles apply. The writer does not have to work as hard at hooking the reader but the writer must still capture the reader's attention. Analyze the letter to see how the structure adheres to the introduction, body, conclusion methodology of writing persuasive cold-call sales letters.

Dear Ms. Bussman:

We hope you were able to see how a PLR air conditioning system would provide energy efficiency, cool comfort, and the maximum return on your investment when we demonstrated the system for you on October 30.

We would like to thank Mr. Lindsay and Mrs. Smooth from your operations division for joining us for the demonstration.

As discussed, the equipment PLR proposes to install is modular in design, so you can add additional units as the need arises. This makes it practical, efficient, and economical, both now and in the future. Therefore, the system protects you against obsolescence as your business continues to grow.

I will follow up on the attached proposal on November 11. The information it provides should answer any pricing and timing questions you might have. However, if you require additional information before November 11, please call me.

In addition, I have attached the results of your free energy efficiency audit showing you 10 no-cost ways to cut your energy bill.

Sincerely,
James P. Callahan
Sales Manager

Proposal cover letter

If your company issues proposals, perhaps in response to a request for quote (RFQ) or a request for proposal (RFP), you should write a proposal cover letter. The sales letter principles apply to proposal cover letters; however, the action you want the reader to take is to read your proposal, not call or buy—at least not until they've read the proposal. The proposal itself will call for a specific action.

Think of your proposal cover letter as you would an executive summary of a report (which we will look at later in the book). Your cover letter is your opportunity to summarize your proposal in a way that motivates the letter reader to read your proposal.

Using the introduction/body/conclusion format, your proposal cover letter (or cover e-mail if you have permission to email your proposal, perhaps as a PDF file) should tell the reader that there is something they need to know in the proposal accompanying your letter or in the attached file.

Many companies write skimpy proposal cover letters or do not include cover letters with proposals. I am not going to say that their proposals will never be read; however, there may be times when a busy executive shoves such proposals to the bottom of the pile or simply bypasses them. In other words, imagine if you had a stack of proposals in front of you, and a limited time to read them. You would glance briefly at the cover letters and separate the proposals that were of interest from those that were not, based on the cover letter. In short, a well-structured, well-written proposal cover letter can motivate the reader to read your proposal.

Let's look at a proposal cover letter (on the next page) set up in full block style. The letter is based on the CAGA Ambrosia apple case study. The CAGA wants to hold a fall fair in New York and Central PR is submitting a bid to manage and promote the event.

Central PR

123 Any Street, Toronto, Ontario M6R 1K7
416.555.1212 - pr@centralpr.com

June 3, 2008

Mr. Johnny McDonald
President
Canadian Apple Growers Association 1
23 McIntosh Boulevard
Milton, Ontario, L6T 1X4

Dear Mr. McDonald:

Take a bite out of the Big Apple—Ambrosia Style!

That is what Central PR proposes to do for the Canadian Apple Growers Association (CAGA) as we promote the exciting New York City unveiling of the Ambrosia apple.

Central PR will promote your Canadian-Style Fall Fair in Central Park and manage the event for you. For one low price, as outlined in the enclosed proposal, we will:

- Write and issue the media release to promote the Fair
- Follow up with the media and compile an accurate list of media attendees
- Create the media kit
- Register and welcome media at the event and arrange interviews with reporters
- Track all media hits connected with your event
- Calculate the media exposure value for the CAGA

You want this event to be as unblemished as the Ambrosia, and Central PR is the agency to ensure the PR for the Fall Fair runs smoothly. Central PR has been in the public relations business since 1999. During this time, we have successfully staged media events in Toronto, Montreal, Vancouver, Los Angeles, and New York City. From fashion to fruit, we have the experience to promote your association.

The enclosed proposal details the program of events and publicity agenda we are proposing for the Canadian-Style Fall Fair. In addition, it includes suggested dates for the event, timelines that will enable you to successfully promote and stage the event, a list of the duties and responsibilities that Central PR will cover on your behalf, a full budget, bios of our executive team and testimonials.

> After you read our Fall Fair proposal, feel free to call me with any questions you may have or to schedule a meeting. We hope to meet by the end of May to discuss this exciting opportunity to represent the CAGA, as the Ambrosia apple makes its New York debut.
>
> Sincerely,
> Nadine Leclair
> Marketing Manager
> Central PR

As the reader, do you feel Central PR understands your promotional objective? Do you fee the PR agency possesses the ability to help you organize and promote an event that will help you achieve your objective? If so, you will read the proposal. If the proposal is sound, and the price is right, you will call and set up a meeting. "Sale" achieved, even though you have not yet bought anything. You would not, in fact, buy this PR service without a meeting. If Central PR is not able to sell you on the concept of the initial meeting, it cannot close the actual sale. In other words, sometimes you have to achieve a preliminary purpose before you can achieve your ultimate purpose. Keep that in mind when you are writing a sales letter or any document.

Sales letter exercise

See if you can put the sales letter writing principles into effect by writing a sales letter or proposal cover letter.

If you don't have anything to write about, but want to try this exercise, produce a sales letter or proposal cover letter based on the Chez Restaurant case study. As with the letter above, pretend that you are a public relations firm responding to a request for proposal to stage the event outlined in the case study. Or you might pretend that you are a PR firm that is seeking new business. Part of your business plan calls for you to develop and pitch PR ideas to companies that have upcoming events—such as the launch of the Ambrosia apple or the opening of Chez Restaurant. In other words, pretend that you have not been asked to submit a proposal but that you are writing a cold call sales letter meant to solicit PR work from CAGA or Chez Restaurant.

Either way, your letter should capture the reader's attention, hold his or her interest, influence the reader's attitude, and cause the reader to take a specific action. Do this with a sales letter that has three distinct sections—introduction, body, and conclusion—and smooth transitions between each section.

Before you start, ask yourself: What's in it for the reader? Your letter should answer that. What is the action that I am trying to motivate? Your letter should build to asking for the order or the action you want to take place.

> **Take some time and outline and write a sales letter or proposal cover letter before you read on.**

Chapter 17: Collaboration and Revision

There is no denying that writing is a personal, solitary task; many business documents, however, benefit from collaborative efforts.

Media releases and other forms of advertising and promotion are often written in collaboration. Consider, for example, an advertising or public relations agency collaborating with a client, or the members of an advertising or public relations agency working together to develop ideas after a client briefing, or the staff of a marketing department working together to develop ideas before writing a brochure or website copy.

The fact is, collaboration can help any writer develop ideas or concepts that can spur the writing. I'd never start a writing job without knowing what I was supposed to write about, the target audience, the type of document I had to produce, and the purpose of the document. Generally, that information comes from my clients; there are times, however, when they ask me how they should approach an issue, and the collaboration begins.

I am not saying writers need to collaborate before writing. However, writers should make conscious decisions about the need to, or not to, collaborate. Often all the elements you need to know before you start to write are not clear. A discussion or meeting with a client, other members of your organization or department, customers, or other stakeholders can help you clarify who you are trying to reach, the specific needs of the audience, the best way to reach the audience, and your true business purpose. Collaboration can also help you develop inventive ideas or solutions to problems and find ways of clearly describing issues or means of requesting assistance or action. These collaborative ideas can help the department, company, or organization speak clearly to its target audience and meet its goals.

In short, the sum of the parts of collaboration can be greater than the whole if collaborators brainstorm in an open and positive environment. Beyond that, sometimes writers formally share decision-making authority on what goes into a document writing and share the writing credit, so you would expect them to collaborate. Often a supervisor or manager has final sign-off authority so, again, you would expect a degree of collaboration with the writer.

Sometimes a document is written by a staff person, revised and approved by a supervisor, and sent to a manager or executive who comments and sends it back down the line for additional revisions. If you have ever worked in government or in other large enterprises, you may be familiar with even more complex versions of the process. This may not be a formal collaborative process; it is often more like a series of edits that often feel subjective to the writer at the bottom of the totem pole. The best advice I can give the writer who sends a document up the ladder and cringes as it comes back down full of red ink or track changes is this: develop a thick skin.

If the people you send the document to have some responsibility for the message, expect change. In fact, if managers, department heads, or senior executives are responsible for signing off on documents, then they should have formal approval processes in place. Respect the process. Work with the feedback you get and improve the document. I've found that you don't always have to make the exact revisions requested (although sometimes you do). More often than not, the revisions inspire in me better ways to write a line or explain a concept. And yes, sometimes I simply look at the revisions, shake my head, and find different ways—not necessarily better, but not worse either—of writing what I have already written.

Why change occurs

The fact is, when a solid first draft is complete, having a second (or even third and fourth) set of eyes reviewing it can help ensure the writer has clearly and logically communicated the agreed-upon message and, of course, can help eradicate the little mistakes and typos that plague so many of us—especially me.

It can be difficult for writers to edit their own work for a number of reasons:

- Writers understand their subject matter so well they often cannot see how or why it is not clear to others
- Writers become so familiar with, or tired of, their work that they skim rather than edit or proofread

Often, however, the suggested (or mandated) revisions feel subjective. So why does subjective change, occur? Sometimes, other people's edits feel subjective, because they are subjective. Some people simply cannot resist the urge to ~~change, revise, edit, alter, modify, adjust, transform, amend, correct, improve, rework, rewrite,~~ *change* another person's copy! Although requested revisions might often seem subjective, or political, in almost every case it is vital to have a pair of fresh eyes review your writing.

In addition, one day you may be in charge and will find that you will not be able to resist the urge to ~~change, revise, edit, alter, modify, adjust, transform, amend, correct, improve, rework, rewrite,~~ *change* another person's copy!

Ease the revision pain

One way to ease the revision pain is to put a formal approval process in place that starts with a discussion between the person who assigns and approves the document and the person who has to write it. This discussion should include the nature and scope of the document, its purpose, the nature and expectations of the audience, and so on—all the elements of the planning part of the writing process. This should help the writer focus on the necessary research. Then the writer should produce a detailed outline and have it reviewed and approved before composing the document.

Let's review some of the benefits of outlining as presented earlier in the book:

- Provides logical structure
- Ensures all major and minor points are covered
- Produces greater clarity and focus
- Helps you detect errors in logic

Imagine producing a detailed outline that your manager approves, or asks you to revise and then approves. A manager who approves a detailed outline is less likely to make structural or substantive changes to a draft that fulfills the expectations of the outline. Yes, the manager might make subjective revisions to your writing; however, I'd rather deal with a few subjective changes than wholesale structural changes. And, since every writer needs an editor, changes—even subjective ones—are not necessarily a bad thing.

Revision and proofreading

Call it my mantra, but allow me to repeat this: every writer needs an editor. If your organization does not have a formal editing and proofreading process in place, try to share important documents with co-workers before you send them out. Solicit comments from others, put on your thick skin, and listen to what others have to say. In fact, take a positive approach. If someone is confused by what you have written and says so, think of that as an opportunity for you to improve your work.

Sometimes, there is nobody around to edit your work. What do you do then? Before you pay attention to grammar and spelling, ask yourself the big-picture document review questions:

- Is my purpose clear?
- Have I covered who, what, where, when, why, how?
- Have I included information the reader requires to act, reply, or decide?
- Have I included too much information?
- Is my message logical and easy to follow?
- Is my writing clear, concise, and focused?
- Will readers understand my vocabulary?
- Are my paragraphs the right length and well organized?
- Have I used the right tone?

What about proofreading?

How do you find and eradicate those little errors you often see after a document has been sent out or is in print? If the document is crucial, consider hiring a freelance editor/proofreader. In fact, if the document is critical, consider hiring a freelance writer who understands your business or at least the sector in which you compete (see the "Send in the writers" section at the end of this chapter for more information).

Here are some practical tips to help you catch and eradicate errors when you have to proofread a document by yourself:

- Give yourself some space between the time you finish writing a solid draft and the time you proof it. The passage of time allows you to take a fresh look at your document and catch any spelling and grammatical errors. Let your document sit overnight, and proofread in the morning when you are fresh.

- Send it to yourself by e-mail first if you can't let a document sit overnight. The process of sending and receiving a document buys you some time, and the process of receiving and opening a document makes it feel newer. This bit of subterfuge will help you catch more errors—as long as you read the document after you open it.

- Read your document aloud. Reading your document out loud slows you down, allowing you to catch mistakes that you would have missed if you were reading silently. They often jump out at you. Also, if a sentence is awkward to read—if you find yourself stumbling as you read it—then it's awkwardly written. Revise.

- Print your document and proofread on paper rather than proofread on the computer screen. Mistakes often jump out at you when you proofread on paper. Pay particular attention to headlines, subheads, formatted fonts (bold and italic type, large type, or colored type), and copy in charts and graphs. The tendency is to scan rather than closely read such formatted type or non-body copy elements of documents. It's amazing how mistakes hide in such places.

- Share your document for peer-editing. Take feedback under advisement. If you ask three people to review a document and two comment on the same passage, that's a sign that you have some revising to do.

- Test your document with selected members of your target audience (if possible). Listen to what those who represent your target readers have to say.

Send in the writers

Sometimes it is worth hiring a freelance writer to write a critical document for you. Imagine that you've been writing all day and you are on your fifth draft of a one-page promotional flyer. You are not sure if the headline will hook your target market. You used affect and spell checker suggested effect, but when you used effect spell checker suggested affect. E-mail is piling up in your in-box. The call answer light on your phone is blinking furiously. And weren't you supposed to set up interviews for the receptionist vacancy? It's time to send in the writers.

Many companies outsource certain business functions, and for good reason. Why spend time doing things that you do not specialize in when you could be closing sales? When it comes to contracting out writing assignments, professional freelance writers can deliver the content you want—on time and on budget.

Just as you do before you contract out any other work, you need to discuss your business requirements and agree on a price for writing work. To help you get the job done right—the right words, on time and on budget—here are five items you should discuss before contracting out writing assignments:

- **Deliverables**: Are you looking for a media release, a one-page flyer, a twenty-minute speech, website copy, promotional e-mail? Define the deliverable to ensure you get what you want.

- **Target Market**: Who are you targeting? Mass-market consumers? Small business owners? Companies in particular sectors? CEOs? Let the writer know whom you are targeting so she can produce words that resonate with your particular target market.

- **Business Image**: Are you a fun and funky company, or are you blue chip? Do you want breezy or solemn copy? Ensure the writer knows the image you want to project so she can strike the right tone.

- **Objective**: What is your purpose? What are you trying to achieve, and why? Are you trying to inform, educate, entertain, or persuade? Do you want a direct response or an eventual response? And what is the response you want? Before writing, the writer needs to know what you want to achieve.

- **Call to Action**: What action do you want the reader to take? For instance, do you want the person reading your brochure to visit your website, call for an appointment, or buy something (if so, how)? The writer needs to know so she can create a clear, concise call to action.

Before the project begins, you should also provide the writer with pertinent background reading material or spend some time discussing your business. If you don't have time to bring the writer up to speed, hire a writer who has written the type of material you need and who understands the nature of your business and the sector in which you operate and/or the sector you are targeting.

How do you know you are getting a professional writer? Read samples on the writer's website or review the writer's portfolio. Also, ask for and check references. In short, do your due-diligence as you would before hiring an employee or any supplier.

Chapter 18: Proposals and Reports

Proposals and reports can be divided into three main sections: front matter, body, and back matter. The list below includes all the elements you might find in each section; however, not all elements have to be included in every report or proposal.

The front matter includes these features:

- Title page
- Abstract
- Table of contents
- List of figures
- Foreword
- Preface
- List of abbreviations and symbols

Most business proposals and reports contain a title page, table of contents, and a list of figures (if tables, charts, and figures are used). A long, formal, research-intensive report might have an abstract or a foreword. Shorter reports, for the most part, will not. Forewords are often used in long, research-intensive reports and are written by a third party, usually someone with some expertise in the area covered by the report, to validate the need for the report or the slant or angle the report takes.

An abstract is a brief summary of a research report or article, thesis, conference proceeding, or any in-depth analysis of a particular subject. It is often used to help readers quickly ascertain the paper's purpose and focus. If there are no abbreviations or symbols used, there would be no need for a list of abbreviations and symbols.

The body includes these features:

- Executive summary
- Introduction
- Text (including headings)

- Conclusion
- Recommendations
- References (or Work Cited)

Almost every report has an executive summary and/or introduction. Reports are often summarized in the executive summary, with an introduction used to spell out the reason for the report and the methodology used to gather information.

When reports do not have forewords and abstracts, some people refer to the text (complete with section subheads) of a report as the body of the report. All that matters, however, is that you include the elements that serve the purpose of the report and the expectations of its readers. Most business proposals and reports also contain a conclusion and/or recommendations (some reports have one or the other; some have both). If no external works are cited, there would be no need for a list of works cited.

The back matter includes these features:

- Appendixes
- Bibliography
- Glossary
- Index

Most business proposals and reports contain appendixes, or more detailed information that supports statements in the report. If works are cited, there might be a bibliography (or footnotes in the report), and if the report is highly technical, it might include a glossary.

Now let's look more closely at some of the more important aspects of proposals and reports.

Title page

As the name implies, this page contains the title of your report. The title should capture the attention of target readers. In most cases, the title page also includes the author's name (or names of the authors) and, if applicable, their title(s) and company or organization. It generally includes a date and may include author contact information and/or a relevant website.

As we have seen, *A Focus on Health Care: Are Canadians Missing an Opportunity?* is not an appropriate title of a report if the report focuses on furniture issues in the health-care industry. If that is the case, this might be a more appropriate report title. *A Focus on the Future of Health-Care Furniture: Are Canadian Manufacturers Missing an Opportunity?*

The report title should strike the proper tone, based on the purpose of the report and the expectations of readers. With tome in mind, *The Ecological Consequences of Diminishing Water Resources in Canada* might be an appropriate title for a scientific or government report. *What Happens When We've Drained Canada Dry?* might make for an interesting headline for a newspaper article that is examining water issues in the country.

Executive summaries, introductions, overviews

As the name implies, the executive summary summarizes the document. In doing so, it should present the purpose of the report or proposal and allude to any conclusion. If you let the reader know up front why you are writing, what you are writing about, and where you are going with it all, the reader will read with your purpose and conclusion in mind. The reader might not agree with everything you write; however, at least he understands the point you are trying to make.

What is the alternative? Leave readers in suspense? Have readers wondering why they are reading, wondering where all this information will take them? If you save your purpose for the end, then readers will have to ponder all that you wrote and determine if, based on the purpose you finally revealed, it all made sense. Now you might think it would be a good thing to have readers ponder all you wrote, but that only works in theory. In fact, if the reader does not understand your purpose from the start, the reader is more likely to abandon your report, or put his or her own interpretation on it.

Like a good headline or report title, the executive summary lets busy readers quickly review the purpose of the report or proposal—what is being addressed and why. For example, if a proposal will help the reader solve a problem, the executive summary would present an overview of the problem and the solution or possible solutions the report will address.

Some people resist giving away so-called trade secrets in an executive summary. All I can say is that when you write a proposal or report, you are not writing a suspense thriller or a murder mystery. Executives do not want to wade through an entire report to get to the good stuff. They want to see it up front; they want you to capture their attention.

Of course, it is your job to also hold interest and influence attitude in the body of your report. And, of course, to hit them with a call to action in your conclusion and/or recommendations. However, you should set them up for that in your executive summary.

Executive summaries are different from introductions. The introduction generally defines the reason the report was written—the issue or opportunity that prompted the writing of the report—and spells out any particular parameters and the methodologies used to gather information for the report.

Although this is true in theory, it isn't always true in practice. In practice, many business writers use the terms executive summary and introduction interchangeably. If you use both, however, the executive summary should detail the purpose of the report and allude to its conclusion or recommendations; the introduction should focus on what motivated the writing of the report and any other relevant background information.

You may come across reports that have executive summaries, overviews and/or introductions, and other preambles. The executive summary might summarize the report and contain recommendations, the overview might give some background information on why the report was commissioned, and the introduction could explain methodologies used in compiling the data in the report.

The point is, if you are writing a report or proposal, at minimum you need to give the reader appropriate background information about what the report was written, summarize the content, and present your purpose. If your report includes recommendations and/or draws conclusions, which almost all reports do, such information is generally summarized in an executive summary that makes a connection between the report's purpose and its conclusion, which is detailed at the end of the report—after your text logically spells out everything the readers need to know to understand the issue so they can act on, or at least agree with, your conclusion and/or recommendations.

Body

This section of a report or proposal offers details such as why a situation exists, how an organization can make it disappear or take advantage of it, other points of view, who should do, or will do, what, when, where, and why—and perhaps how.

The body—divided into defined sections, each with its own subhead (relating to the major topic points in your outline)—works to fulfill the purpose stated in the executive summary and makes clear the rationale for any conclusion or recommended actions. It must hold the interest of the reader, influence the reader's attitude, and ask for, suggest, or recommend specific actions.

To influence attitude, the body of the report might spell out any possible benefits taking a particular course of action will lead to and raise, and overcome, any objections readers might have. In addition, to make the report feel comprehensive and objective, part of the body might examine positions that are contrary to the slant of the report, such as costs/benefits of not taking recommended actions or costs/benefits of alternative actions. The body might also include a detailed schedule (timelines indicating who is responsible for what during each phase of the project, for instance) and a detailed projection of costs (proposed budget), and other relevant elements.

Conclusion/Recommendations

The main purpose of the conclusion is to restate, in a summary, the body (text) of the report, while logically concluding where the body leads the reader. It spells out that conclusion for the reader and may serve to set up any specific recommendations, which should spring logically from the conclusion.

The conclusion reinforces the salient points of the document—the points you want readers to take away or the points you want them to remember—even if they forget everything else they have read. It also hammers home the points that you, the writer, hope will lead to action, however you have defined the action: the change in policy, increase in budget, launch of a new campaign, acceptance of the bid, and so on. That may be done in the recommendation section.

As the name implies, the recommendation section lists recommendations the writer wants the reader to consider or implement. If there are no recommendations, a report would have a conclusion; however, if there are recommendations, the report could have both a conclusion section and a recommendation section.

On the next page you will find an example of a conclusion followed by several recommendations:

Conclusion

On average, customer service representatives leave the company within nine months of hiring. To break even on its investment in training, the company must find ways to keep new customer service representatives on the job for at least one year, so the company is not losing money on employee training and is not paying exorbitant recruitment costs to fill each vacancy. If this issue is not resolved, the company will have to increase product prices; however, such action will make the company less competitive in an increasingly competitive market.

Recommendations

To increase the return on investment for training new customer service representatives, the committee proposes that the following three recommendations be implemented within three months:
1. Recommendation one....
2. Recommendation two....
3. Recommendation three....

Repetition is your friend

Does it sound as if there are similarities between the executive summary and the conclusion? And does it sound as if the body or text of the report is simply a detailed elaboration of the executive summary? If it helps, think of it this way:

- The executive summary tells the readers what you are going to tell them.
- The body tells the readers what you said you were going to tell them.
- The conclusion tells the readers what you told them.

Why the repetition in proposals and reports? I don't want to say that readers are lazy, but they often are. Most likely, though, they are busy. This repetition helps them determine how much they should read while understanding what you are saying, even if they don't read the full report.

When you purchased your computer, printer, or cellular phone, you probably received a thick manual (or detailed PDF file), a quick-start guide, and perhaps an illustrated set-up guide. All three documents include similar information, but the thick manual goes into much more detail and has additional background information. If you are like me, you used the illustrated guide (the shortest document) first. If that didn't help, you turned to the quick-start manual. If that left some questions unanswered, you sighed and opened the manual. However, if you wanted to know everything you need to know about your device before you start to work with it (there really are people like that out there), you might have turned to the manual first.

Executives and other decision makers tend to be busy people. The executive summary (quick-start manual) helps them determine how important the document is—to them, not to you. It helps them determine when, or if, they will read the full document or manual, or at least browse through relevant sections or possibly jump to the conclusion and recommendations.

In addition, not all people who receive reports need to read them from beginning to end. The synopsis keeps in the loop those who are peripherally interested in the topic. If someone strongly agrees or disagrees with an executive summary, they might read the entire document or they might pass it on to another person who can read it and reply on their behalf, or take (or counter) the recommendation actions.

Deciding which elements to include

When it comes to deciding which elements you should use in a report, and when you should use them, your choices depend on the topic, your audience, their knowledge of the situation and overall expectations, the amount of necessary research that went into the report (some people do to much research, others don't do enough, and some do the right amount), and the detail you need to persuade your audience to act. (Also, politics might come into play, but a discussion about the politics that may be involved in report writing goes beyond the scope of this book.)

If your report is longer than five pages, for instance, you will probably have a table of contents. There is a school of thought that PDFs longer than three pages should have a table of contents. PDFs are often read on screen and the reader, not holding anything tangible in hand, can use the table of contents, which has page numbers, to determine how much time it will take to read the report (as well as to determine if the content is relevant). In short, the table of contents for a PDF serves as a content overview; however, using a table of contents does not preclude the use of an executive summary and/or introduction.

If you are writing an authoritative report and want or need to have a higher authority validate it, you might ask said higher authority to read your report and write a foreword.

If you are writing a technical report for a business or political audience, you will store much of the technical material in the appendixes so that your readers do not get bogged down in technical minutiae. If you use a number of technical terms, you will include a glossary.

If you cite no other works in your report, you will not need to include a reference or works cited section. And so it goes.

Introduction and executive summary samples

On the next couple of pages, you will find several examples of introductions and executive summaries from various reports and proposals. It can be difficult to understand the purpose of a report if you are not the intended audience; however, see if you can determine why each introduction or executive summary was written (the purpose) and what it is summarizing. In addition, see if you can determine the conclusion or the call to action.

As you read, ask yourself the following questions:

- Does the writing capture my attention and hold my interest? It's one thing if it does not because you are not the intended audience; it's another if it does not because the writing is ineffective.
- Is the writing clear, concise, coherent, and focused?
- Are the sentences grouped logically into paragraphs that present one primary idea? Do the ideas unfold in a logical order?

Hosted e-commerce anyone?

The first executive summary is from a white paper, or research-intensive report. It is targeted at companies that are thinking of implementing electronic commerce, or e-commerce, solutions and is focused on the advantages of "hosted e-commerce." It is not trying to sell a particular brand of e-commerce; it is just looking at the viability of the hosted e-commerce option. Instead of building and hosting an e-commerce website, product ordering systems, and transaction processing systems, some companies farm this work out to third parties who specialize in building and hosting such systems. When it comes to hosted e-commerce, issues such as security and privacy are often a concern, however. In addition, some companies fear a loss of control—they fear losing the ability to update and customize their websites, for instance—if they outsource e-commerce to a third party. Hosting an e-commerce system requires capital expenditures and in-house expertise. And, ironically, issues such as security and privacy are still a concern.

Hosted E-commerce:
Building Competitive Advantages for Online Retailers

Executive Summary

In an intensely competitive Web-based online sales environment, e-commerce retailers are constantly in search of ways to increase sales, acquire new customers, improve reliability and security, and reduce technology costs. The result is a market-wide demand for enhanced e-commerce technology, effectively paving the way for a new breed of hosted e-commerce solutions.

By bridging the gap between the control and customization provided by e-commerce solutions that companies build or buy, roll-out, and host internally, and the cost-effectiveness and rapid market access provided by hosted solutions, next generation hosted e-commerce presents significant value for online retailers. These new hosted platforms elevate the e-commerce experience through customizable inventory and order management, distribution, branding, reliability, and reduced overall cost.

Next generation hosted e-commerce solutions enable enterprises and mid-market online sellers to create new revenue streams, acquire new customers, and simplify online selling—while controlling costs and maintaining 7/24 up-time through a hosted e-commerce provider.

So will the reader outsource e-commerce?

While there is no overt purpose statement, the purpose is quite clear: to educate the reader about hosted e-commerce. We can presume the reader is knows about e-commerce and typical e-commerce solutions because there is no general introduction to the history of, and need for, e-commerce. By the end of the executive summary, the reader knows the benefits of hosted e-commerce and the conclusion of the report—that large enterprises and mid-market companies should consider host e-commerce.

Notice, however, just as the executive summary does not use the word "purpose," it does not use the word "conclusion." In other words, you want to convey your purpose and your conclusion when writing, but you don't need to explicitly flag those points.

To the point

The introduction below is from a response to a request for proposal (RFP) looking for quotes on an e-mail writing seminar. Notice how specific the start of the proposal is. The writer can get away with this since the proposal is a reply to a specific request—a request for an e-mail writing seminar.

Proposal:
To-The-Point: Effective E-mail Writing Seminar

Executive Summary

If you want to become a more effective and efficient e-mail writer—writing e-mail messages that get to the point—then the "To-The-Point" writing seminar is for you. During the seminar, you will learn how to plan, structure, and write concise, effective e-mail messages that make your point and motivate your reader to take appropriate, timely action.

Studies show that efficient writers follow the writing process. They spend as much of their time planning as they do writing, and they understand the importance of reviewing and editing messages before sending them. This seminar will outline the writing process and show participants how to apply it to original e-mail messages and e-mail replies. In addition, it will demonstrate why effective e-mail messages capture attention (starting with the subject line), hold interest, influence attitude, and ask for action.

The 3-hour seminar detailed in this proposal includes theory, practical advice, hints, and tips, sample messages, writing exercises, and feedback. The 6-hour seminar described here includes more samples and additional writing exercises with more extensive feedback.

Is my future bright?

It always amazes me that some companies really don't know how they are doing and don't know what their prospects are. Companies often have to call in consultants to help them figure out how they are doing and how they can improve what they are doing. The consultants have to conduct research, analyze the data, and, of course, write a report.

Prospects for Outdoor Equipment Ltd.

Introduction

This report provides an analysis and evaluation of the current and prospective profitability, liquidity, and financial stability of Outdoor Equipment Inc.

Methods of analysis include trend, horizontal, and vertical analyses as well as ratios such as Debt, Current, and Quick ratios. Other calculations include rates of return on Shareholders' Equity and Total Assets and Earnings per Share, to name a few. All calculations can be found in the appendixes.

Results of data analyzed show that all ratios are below industry averages. In particular, comparative performance is poor in the areas of profit margins, liquidity, credit control, and inventory management.

The report finds the prospects of the company, in its current position, are not positive. The major areas of weakness require further investigation and remedial action by management. However, preliminary recommendations that will enable the company to move towards profitability are included.

Recommendations discussed include:
1. improving the average collection period for accounts receivable,
2. improving/increasing inventory turnover, and
3. reducing pre-payments and perhaps increasing inventory levels.

Buddy can you spare a dime?

When companies want to raise funds for new ventures, they have to produce a prospectus that tells potential investors what the company is proposing to do and why it will be profitable. Since this report is going out to potential investors who may not be keenly aware of how the restaurant industry operates, let alone why a Web portal would be a good idea, the report starts with some general information. The start, however, is directly related to the restaurant industry and quickly moves to the idea of the portal.

Prospectus:
ABC Inc. Develops Web 2.0 Restaurant Portal

Executive Summary

Currently, restaurant owners decide on the food they want to offer, create menus, open their doors, and hope people will drop in or make reservations.

Some restaurants advertise in local media or mail out flyers within the local community. A number have websites that let potential customers view menus and look up contact information. A few restaurants take reservations online, generally by e-mail, to better serve customers. However, many small and family-owned restaurants don't have websites, let alone have sites that take e-mail reservation—never mind an automated reservation process. And no restaurants gather information about customers that would allow them to tailor menus to customer desires.

There is an opportunity for ABC Inc. to provide a Web 2.0 portal that would enable small and family-owned restaurants across North America to provide potential customers with searchable menus, location and contact information, and automated reservation systems—while gathering demographic information, price range and food preference, and other pertinent data about customers.

Such business intelligence could be shared in an aggregate, non-competitive manner with all restaurants that belonged to the portal and enable restaurateurs to better plan menus, offer specials, and market services.

This model is based on a philosophy of users providing voluntary information so ABC Inc. can provide restaurants with business intelligence that will enable them to improve customer service and satisfaction. For example, by using the portal, restaurants can know their customers' food, seating, and other preferences are as soon as they make a reservation

Using the food service industry as an entrance into the business intelligence market, ABC Inc. plans on developing a variety of portals for the hospitality and tourism industry. These portal services will transform ABC Inc. into a "super concierge" company. However, ABC Inc. is taking a phased implementation approach, looking to raise investment funding to first create a restaurant-industry Web portal, before expanding its portal offering.

Buddy can you spare a freelance writer?

Companies that hire freelance writers often issue RFPs. Writers then have to respond with proposals. You can't just say, "This is what it will cost." The proposal has to demonstrate the writer understands the needs of the potential client, and has the ability and experience to deliver the writing, before the client will consider hiring the writer. In other words, the job will not necessarily go to the lowest bidder; it will go to the bidder who demonstrates the greatest understanding of what the clients needs and the ability to deliver the goods—as long as the writer's quote is within the client's budget.

Magic Moment Greeting Cards
Business Plan Writing Proposal

Executive Summary

This proposal outlines the components of traditional business plans and lays out a general marketing framework that will enable a manufacturer of a consumer product, such as Magic Moment, to target both retail and consumer markets. A detailed business plan, one that includes an extensive marketing plan component, written for Magic Moment by PLC Inc. would enable the company to organize, manage, and focus its business, marketing, and sales efforts to achieve maximum return on investment and effort.

Magic Moment Greeting Cards manufactures two categories of unique greeting cards—a CD card and a recordable card. To date, Magic Moment has developed six lines for different markets. Based on market research, Magic Moment knows that consumers and store owners have a high appreciation of its products.

Magic Moment has the sales force in place to sell the product across Canada and in the U.S.A. The company is looking for a business writer with marketing expertise to put together a business plan—a strategic plan of action that will enable Magic Moment to generate the maximum profit by wholesaling the product to retail outlets and by supporting retail sales with business-to-consumer advertising and promotion.

Magic Moment requires a detailed Business Plan that includes a comprehensive and creative business-to-business and business-to-consumer Marketing Plan.

PLC Inc.'s team of writers can deliver that plan for $5,000 based on the defined purpose and scope of the project detailed in this proposal.

Will PLC land the job?

In five paragraphs, has PLC captured Magic Moment's attention and held the reader's interest? If so, the proposal will be read. If not, it won't be. If PLC demonstrates an understanding of Magic Moments writing needs and PLC's ability to meet those needs, and if the quoted price is right, PLC will land the job. If the price is right but the proposal is not read, or does not say what Magic Moments needs to hear, PLC will not land the job. In some ways, it is that simple. And yes, at times it is more complex than that. The fact remains, however, if your writing is not read, nothing will happen. So write to be read.

Where do we go from here?

Ideally, the introduction and executive summary are the last two sections of the report that you write because you cannot summarize something that has not be written. At the same time, if you produce a detailed outline, it is possible to write your executive summary and/or introduction before you write the body or text portion of your report. So it's not so much a matter of where you go from here, as much as it is a matter of how did you get to your executive summary. At the risk of repeating myself (although repetition is your friend in business writing), you start with knowing your topic, purpose, and audience. You then do applicable research and you create a detailed outline. Then you write.

When outlining reports, I like to create a major topic point (what the report is all about), followed by a series of section points, equivalent to the subheads in a chapter of this book. Then I list the subpoints, secondary points, and tertiary points under each section point. There really is no point in starting the actual writing until the outline is complete. So where you go from here is you continue to follow the writing process, only you follow a more extensive process than you use for writing e-mail messages and letters—particularly in terms of the research and the outline process.

You will also find the more extensive the scope of the document and the longer it is, the more time you will spend revising and polishing it; however, if you try to write it before you research and outline it, you will spend even more time writing your first draft and revising the document.

Executive summary writing exercise

If you have a report or proposal to write, it is my hope that what you have read here will help you tackle a first draft. If you want to tackle a report-writing exercise, you can try the exercises below. On the other hand, if you want to read more about writing executive summaries before you try the exercises or start your own project, read the next chapter on specific versus general.

Remember the media release you wrote, based on the case studies presented in the media release writing chapter of the book? If you want to write proposals based on the case studies, here is what you can do: pretend you represent a public relations firm that hopes to plan and implement one of the events outlined in the case studies, and write a proposal.

Companies frequently contract out the planning and implementation of publicity events to public relations firms. Usually the company knows what they want to promote, but they do not know how to promote it. So, they send out an RFP to at least three companies. The RFP says something like this:

> This is who we are, this is whom we want to reach through the media, and this is why we want to reach them. Therefore, propose an event that would help us reach our audience through the media. Give us your rationale for this event and the cost for staging it. In other words, tell us what you suggest we do and tell us why you think we should do it—why it would work—and how much it is going to cost us. And tell us why we should trust you to pull it off.

If you want to practice, pretend you have been asked to help one of the companies or organizations in the media-release writing case studies generate some PR and write a proposal. You can use the PR events outlined in the media-release writing chapter as the foundation for what you are going to propose to do.

The goal here is to follow these steps:

- Think about what you want to say and how you will say it.
- Outline your proposal.
- Write the proposal, including an introduction and executive summary.
- Edit and proofread your work.

Before you begin your exercise, I suggest you take a moment to outline the following:

- Why you are writing (your purpose).
- Whom you are writing for (the PR company).
- Whom you will target with the PR event (both in terms of media and the target market for the product or service you will be promoting).
- What you are planning to do to attract media attention, and why (rationale for the event).
- Whom you will invite to this event: media only, or media and selected guests (representing your target market), or media, selected guests and/or the general public.
- Where this event will take place and your rationale for the location.
- When it will take place and your rationale for the date, season, time.
- Why it will take place—why it will attract media attention and why it will appeal to your target market.

You might have noticed several whys in the above outline. It is deliberate. Although the five Ws are the foundation of any writing, why is at the heart of the foundation. And often there are multiple whys at the heart. So before you write anything, ask yourself who, what, where, when, and why, why, why.

The reply to a RFQ would include a cover letter and a full proposal. For this exercise, all you need to do is think about what you would put in the body or text of the proposal:

- Introduction
- Executive summary
- Problem or opportunity
- Proposed solution and rationale
- Timelines
- Budget
- About your company (why you are the company to do it)
- Conclusion and/or recommendations

A full proposal would also include the other elements of a report described in this chapter, such as a cover page and table of contents. The text would also include things like bios of company executives, testimonials from previous clients, and other information required to help the PR land the deal.

At the same time, if you've never staged a PR event, it might be difficult to create a budget for one or detail the timelines, so feel free to skip those sections.

Outline a proposal. Try to write the body of a proposal, before you read on.

Chapter 19: Specific Versus General

When it comes to writing a report or proposal, the writing does not occur until you have done the following:

- Preparation
- Research
- Organization

It is amazing how many people, when given a complex writing assignment, will simply turn on their computers and begin to write. As you know by now, before you begin any writing—short or long, simple or complex—I suggest you follow the writing process outlined in this book.

For short e-mail and memos, answering the W5 questions—who, what, where, when, and why—might be all the preparation, research, and organization you need. For longer, formal reports, you should not start to write until you have gone through stages one and two of the process, and then produced a detailed outline.

Once you have an outline in place, you can write from point to point and complete a first draft before you revise. If you really need to edit before you finish writing—in other words, if you cannot move forward knowing that there are typos, grammatical errors, or less than fully coherent sentences in your document—then at least finish one section of your report or proposal before you do any editing. That way you are editing a block of writing that, in theory, is complete in itself.

General to specific or specific to general?

But where should you, or how should you, start to write? Should you start with a general overview or plunge into specific details?

If your reader knows little about the topic, or if you have to educate before you can influence or persuade, start with a general introduction to the topic and lead up to the specific details required to achieve your purpose. However, if your reader is intimately familiar with the topic and needs to know how to solve a problem or take advantage of an opportunity, you can get right to the point by starting with the specifics.

Starting with related generalities or specific conditions is really a guideline as most reports include some background information to put the topic in a business context before they get to the specifics.

For instance, say you are writing a report for senior executives about e-commerce that recommends your company invest $750,000 and hire five new staff members to implement an e-commerce-enabled website so it can sell products online. Senior executives read *The Wall Street Journal, The Globe and Mail,* and other business publications. They are quite familiar with e-commerce. Being senior executives, they also would know if their company had an e-commerce-enabled website, and if it was producing revenue at a profit.

Your goal, as the writer, is to determine whether you should start with the specifics, or start with the general and move to the specific. In other words, do you give your audience some context before you get on with the specifics?

Let's say the company is one of the last in its sector to get into e-commerce. Some specific context might be advisable—what has been happening in the sector and what has held the company back. In other words, you would not want to be so general as to present the history of e-commerce to your audience.

On the other hand, let's say it was 1998 and the company was the first one in its sector to think about taking the e-commerce plunge. Providing some general context about the Internet—how pervasive it is becoming and how it is being used as a sales tool in some sectors—before you get to the specifics would be advisable. At the same time, you would not want to give the full history of the Internet. That would be too general.

In other words, in both cases, you have to give your reader enough contextual information to set the stage, before you move to the detailed specifics of the situation. Sometimes, though, setting the stage involves far less background information than at other times; sometimes, you have much less work to do to bring your reader up to speed.

Say, for instance, you are a senior marketing executive with a firm that manufactures machines and parts for the pulp and paper industry. Sales for your company, as they are for the entire industry, are stagnant. You have been asked to propose ways to boost revenue. You have been given a green light to blue-sky (if I am allowed to mix my metaphors and colors). After conducting extensive research, you conclude that the company should expand its operations by delivering services—systems integration, training, consulting, and so on—that would help the pulp and paper industry cut costs and make it more efficient, and open a new business line for your company.

This is known as a *paradigm shift*—a significant change from one fundamental view to another—and you would not want to spring this upon your reader without outlining the economic, competitive, and other relevant conditions in your industry. (Although this is starting with the general, notice how it still relates to your industry.) Then you would present your thinking (the specifics) as to the new course of action the company should take. The general, leading up to the specific, would be spelled out in brief in your executive summary. The body of the report would give detailed general background before addressing the specifics of the report, all supported by your research, data, and projections.

To illustrate the concept further, let me use a non-business scenario featuring Stephen Lewis, one of Canada's most respected commentators on social affairs, international development, and human rights. In 2001, U.N. Secretary-General Kofi Annan appointed Mr. Lewis as his special envoy for HIV/AIDS in Africa. In April 2005, *Time* named him one of the one hundred most influential people in the world.

When Stephen Lewis talked about AIDS in Africa to a knowledgeable and supportive audience on World AIDS day, December 1, 2005, he got right to the point. In fact, he even started his speech by telling his audience that he was going to get right to the point. He put forward two specific proposals (telling his audience what he was going to tell them). Here are the opening two paragraphs of his speech:

> There are many occasions during the course of the year to pronounce about the pandemic. On the occasion of this World AIDS Day, I'd like to resist the temptation to run with hyperbole. Rather, I'd like to put two specific proposals which may seem obvious, but which speak, I believe, to the heart of the struggle against the virus.

> The first involves dollars. The Global Fund to Fight AIDS,
> Tuberculosis, and Malaria—the best financial vehicle by
> far to help break the back of the pandemic—is in terrible
> trouble. It is over three billion dollars short for 2006 and
> 2007, and that shortfall will doom millions to death in
> the following years unless something drastic is done,
> and fast.

Now, for contrast, look at how he started his speech to the Global Health Council's Annual Conference, May 28, 2003. The Global Health Council, the world's largest membership alliance dedicated to saving lives by improving health throughout the world, is concerned about AIDS and many other health-related issues. Here is how Stephen Lewis opened his remarks:

> I sometimes think that the continent I love, and the
> continent to which my U.N. role is devoted—Africa—is
> under some kind of other-worldly curse. So many factors
> conspire against it that one could imagine inexplicable
> forces at work, except that we know, we emphatically
> know, that every factor haunting Africa has a quite
> straightforward explanation. It's the relationship
> amongst the factors that we sometimes fail to under-
> stand. What I therefore want to do in this speech is to
> make the connections and attempt to demonstrate that
> Africa reaps what the world sows, and with a vengeance.

Notice how he still tells you what he is going to tell you. However, he is much more general (within the topic he is discussing) in his approach. In other words, starting with the general is not starting with a digression. He is still very much on topic as he brings his audience up to speed. In fact, Mr. Lewis goes on for several more paragraphs before he gets to the specifics— the factors and forces at work.

So where do you start your reports? With your topic, audience and their expectations and knowledge, and your purpose in mind. Let that guide where you start your writing.

Chapter 20: Feasibility Reports, Evaluations, Appraisals

As mentioned, there are many types of reports and proposals. In this chapter, we examine two types of common reports—feasibility reports and evaluations.

Feasibility reports

Companies and organizations seldom take any action until they know if it is feasible to do so.

Launch a new product? Is there a need for it? What will it cost to produce and market? What can we charge for it? What is the competition up to? How many units will we sell in years one, two, three, four, five? When do we (do we?) start to generate a profit?

The plant can't keep up with orders? Should we increase production capacity? Is it more feasible to expand the existing plant or build a new one? If the latter, where should we locate the new plant? Which city (country?) is the most feasible one in which to locate our plant? That would depend on a number of factors, would it not?

Feasibility reports include sections with which you are now familiar—introduction, body, conclusion, and recommendation. The introduction of a feasibility report presents background information and outlines the scope of the report—answering the questions as to why this report is necessary and how detailed it will be. The executive summary, as the name implies, summarizes the report and gives an indication of what the outcome of the report will be. In other words, it lets the reader know if the project is feasible and if the company or organization should embark on it.

The body presents a look at the pros and cons of the various factors taken under consideration as well as any alternatives. The conclusion tends to point to the most feasible option, but it might present a variety of options or recommend further study. The recommendation(s), supported by the body and conclusion, spell out the suggested action. On the other hand, the recommendation may deviate from the facts presented in the body and the conclusion based on external factors—political or environmental, for instance as in this example:

Conclusion
The most timely and cost-effective way to build the new eight-lane highway connecting Metropolis with Urbanitis would be to cut through the Rouge River Valley Ravine. However, as outlined, that is not the most environmentally friendly or politically expedient approach.

Recommendation
While the least expensive way to build the new eight-lane highway connecting Metropolis with Urbanitis would be to cut through the Rouge River Valley Ravine, the environmental impact would be devastating, as would the political outcry. Therefore, it is recommended that the Ministry of Transportation spend an additional two billion dollars and take an additional five years to... yada, yada, yada...

Such a recommendation should not come unexpectedly. The report must—in the body—address the details that lead to the recommendation and must—in the executive summary—indicate that those factors will be considered in the report. Notice even how the conclusion alludes to potential problems if the most cost-effective approach is taken.

Evaluations and appraisals

Evaluations and appraisals are used to gather, analyze, and disseminate information. Performance, product, and/or customer service appraisals and evaluations are an important part of many businesses. They help businesses determine if manufacturing systems are meeting efficiency standards, if products are meeting quality standards, if employees are working up to expectations and achieving stated goals, if customer service levels are meeting and exceeding customer demands, and if business processes are functioning as intended.

If the appraisal system reveals problems or issues, then management can take corrective action before the problem or issue becomes a black hole that sinks the organization.

For instance, people are evaluated to establish and maintain high levels of performance among employees and to enhance management effectiveness in making decisions that influence the coordination of human resources. Employees who fail performance appraisals can be offered advice, training, or counseling. Employees who consistently fail the appraisal process can be reassigned or terminated—as long as due process has been followed.

To ensure high levels of quality are maintained, products are continually evaluated. If manufacturing or production flaws are detected or if suppliers are shipping parts that do not meet quality standards, companies can act to avoid or minimize customer complaints, costly recalls, and legal problems over safety and other issues.

Companies evaluate customer service levels to ensure that staff members are meeting or exceeding customer expectations. Satisfied customers (those who have had their expectations met or exceeded) are likely to become repeat customers. On the other hand, dissatisfied customers tell friends and relatives about service problems. They even use the Internet—websites, blogs, and social media primarily—to share their negative experiences with the world.

Service evaluations enable companies to offer additional staff training or to improve customer service processes, as may be required.

To reveal an accurate picture, the performance of people, products, services, and systems must be evaluated based on predetermined expectations and measured against specific criteria or standards. To avoid subjectivity, the criteria or standards must be measurable (although that may not be possible in all cases). In addition, the criteria must reflect the person, product, service, or system in context: the person in relation to his or her position, the product in relation to the manner in which it should be used, the service in relation to service delivery expectations, and so on.

Appraisals and evaluations can be complex processes. No matter how complex the process is, however, it ends in a written report. Before writing the report, specific pre-evaluation questions about whatever is under evaluation must be answered. Before producing the questions and gathering the data, however, the evaluator must know basic information, such as:

- What is the business purpose of performing the evaluation?
- Who or what is under evaluation?

- What are the performance expectation standards/criteria against which you base your evaluation?
- How much weight do you give each expectation factor?
- What questions do you ask to perform an effective evaluation?
- Who receives the evaluation report? Why?
- Based on the evaluation, who recommends the action to take, or takes it?
- How do you write up the evaluation?
- What follow-up evaluation is required? When?

Without answers to those questions, it would be impossible to begin the evaluation or appraisal process. With that theory in mind, let's put the process into practice.

Evaluate the book so far

Let's perform a simple evaluation of this book. Before we evaluate the book, we need to answer the above questions. Allow me to help set up the evaluation by proving my take on the answers to the questions, which you are free to revise. If you would actually like to evaluate the book and send me your thoughts, feel free to write up a short evaluation report based on the work we are going to do here and send it to info@paullima.com. (I can't guarantee that I will reply to all e-mail that I receive; however, I will read all evaluations and take comments under advisement when I work on the next edition of the book.)

Here is my take on how you can answer the pre-evaluation questions:

What is the business purpose of performing the evaluation? The business purpose of the evaluation is to help the author improve the book. (On the other hand, you might feel it is to allow the reader to express frustration or appreciation.)

Who or what is under evaluation? Harness the Business Writing Process.

What are the performance expectation standards/criteria against which you base your evaluation? It is expected that this book will help readers write more effective e-mail messages, letters, reports, and Web copy—ideally in a more efficient manner. The expectations have been established through marketing messages and the book title. For students using this book as a textbook, expectations may have been established in part by a course description or course outline.

Note: The above criteria may feel subjective. To an extend they are, as are many aspects of evaluations. It is your job to look for important criteria, subjective or otherwise. In addition, you should try to find objective criteria. In the case of this book, you might look at availability of the book, cost of the book, concepts discussed, clarity of the writing, and technical level of the book. Again, there may be a subjective take on some of these criteria, but it is your job to set the standards, ask the questions, and measure the results.

How much weight do you give each expectation factor? Based on your expectations, you would add other criteria to the above list, revise or remove criteria, and rank criteria from most important to least important. If the book meets your most important criteria, but not your least important criteria, it could be considered a success with some room for improvement. Of course, if it does not meet your important criteria, it would be deemed a failure—even if it met some of your secondary criteria.

What questions do you ask to perform an effective evaluation (based on your criteria)?

- After completing the book and exercises presented, are you a more effective writer? Are you a more efficient writer?
- Was the book easy to obtain?
- Was the cost of the book reasonable, compared to similar books?
- Were the concepts discussed in the book appropriate, considering the book marketing material and the title of the book?
- Is the writing clear, concise, and focused?
- Is the technical level of the content appropriate to the subject matter and the learning needs of most who would read this book?

Who receives the evaluation report? The author could receive the evaluation. Conceivably, the publisher could receive it. If you wrote up your evaluation as a book review, it could be sent to a newspaper or magazine. If you are part of a class using the book as a textbook, the course instructor or course administrator could receive your evaluation.

Based on the evaluation, who recommends the action to take, or takes it? This depends on who receives the evaluation. For instance, if the author receives it, he could revise the book, if required. An instructor or course administrator could recommend using the book again, or not using it.

How do you write up the evaluation? The evaluation could simply be a list of questions with answers on a scale of one to five. However, if you want to convey your analysis in a way that best helps those who need to understand your evaluation, you would write a report that included an introduction, executive summary, body, conclusion, and recommendation(s).

Of course, you could also write a review of the book for a blog, magazine, or newspaper. A review is not a formal report and writing reviews goes beyond what the scope of this book. If you were to read book reviews, however, you'd see that they tend to start with an overview or synopsis of the book being reviewed, present details of what worked and what did not, and why, and then wrap up with a conclusion or recommendation. Often, the review lead (opening or introductory paragraphs) foreshadows (gives you a sense of) the conclusion. In other words, they are structured like reports but not formatted like them, and the language tends to be less formal.

What follow-up evaluation is required? When? In this case, there is no follow up required. In theory, though, the author could revise the book and send it to you for a second evaluation or continue to receive evaluations from readers. In more complex corporate situations, follow-up evaluations are scheduled to determine if the recommendations have been acted upon and if those actions have produced the desired effects.

Answer your evaluation questions

Once you have determined what your evaluation criteria and questions should be, you answer them. If you were evaluating customer service, you would find a means of surveying customers so they could answer your questions. If you were evaluating a product, you might implement a quality control system that lets you evaluate product quality before you ship your product to customers.

If you are evaluating this book, you could read it and evaluate it. For your evaluation to be more effective, however, it would make sense to try the exercises and compare your writing after reading the book to your writing before reading the book.

Once you have answered your evaluation questions, you should be able to write your report. Think of your answers as research material—the material that will help you outline what you want to write in your report. You can then organize your answers to produce an outline for your report. With your research done and your outline completed, all that is left for you to do is to write the evaluation.

If you produce a formal evaluation report, your title and executive summary should capture attention. The body should hold interest as it elaborates on the executive summary. It should also influence attitude based on the persuasive logic of your writing. In addition, the body of your report could be subdivided into distinct sections based on your criteria and expectations.

Keep your reader in mind as you write. The reader needs to know you had some evaluation standards or the reader may feel that you are simply spouting a subjective opinion. That does not mean there will be no subjectivity in your report; however, detailing your criteria and expectations will make the report feel more objective and authoritative.

The conclusion should summarize your report and set up the recommendations, if you have any. (I'd be surprised if you did not.)

Borrow or revise the above evaluation questions and write an evaluation report (or at least an executive summary). Feel free to submit it to info@paullima.com. I will read all evaluations received; if I have time, I will reply.

> You can evaluate the book now or wait until you finish reading it before you evaluate it. Feel free to submit your evaluation to info@paullima.com.

Chapter 21: Writing for the Web

When it comes to surfing the Web, scanning is the new reading. Most Web surfers scan Web pages; few read Web pages word by word.

Reading on a monitor (even a high-resolution one) is more difficult than reading well-designed printed material. Most people read slower on monitors (versus reading printed material), so they scan to compensate for the extra time is takes to read. You want the copy on your website to capture attention, hold interest, influence attitude, and motivate action, but you also have to make Web pages easy to scan or people will simply leave your website.

There are a number of ways to make Web pages easy to scan, as we shall see. However, let's first look at some copy and review its readability (or scanability) quotient.

When I wrote material for the home page of my website, I could have written promotional copy using full sentences and a full paragraph, like this:

> Based in Toronto, Paul Lima is a veteran freelance writer and business writing trainer. He has been a freelance writer, copywriter, and business-writing instructor for over 25 years. He offers large enterprises, small businesses, and organizations a variety of effective business writing and copywriting services and powerful business-writing training seminars. His quality business writing includes case studies, copywriting (brochures, sales letter, and other promotional material), Web content, media releases, proposals, and reports. His proven business-training seminars include business writing and media interview preparation. In addition, he has written several powerful, practical books on topics such as business writing, media release writing, and copywriting. Finally, for freelancer writers, Paul offers cost-effective seminars, e-courses, books and e-books, and free, stimulating content on his blog.

Now let's look at the same passage written in what one might describe as a more objective manner—in other words, with the more promotional elements removed.

> Based in Toronto, Paul has been a freelance writer, copywriter, and business-writing instructor for over 25 years. He offers companies and organizations business writing and copywriting services and business-writing training seminars. His business writing includes case studies, copywriting, Web content, media releases, proposals, and reports. His business training seminars include business writing and media interview preparation. In addition, he has written several books on business writing, media release writing, and copywriting. Finally, Paul offers freelance writers seminars, e-courses, books and e-books, and blog posts.

Web-based tests show that more objective passages, like the one above, are easier to absorb than more promotional passages because people read Web copy differently than they read paper-based documents. That does not make the above passage ideally suited for the Web. And if website visitors are abandoning your copy, no matter how well it is written, it is ineffective.

Readability tests, like one conducted by Jakob Nielsen (*How Users Read on the Web*, Jakob Nielsen's Alertbox), analyze Web passages based on the following factors:

- **Task time**: Time it takes visitors to find answers to questions pertaining to the text.
- **Memory**: What visitors retain after reading.
- **Errors**: Number of incorrect answers users give for questions that have known answers.
- **Time to recall site structure**: Number of seconds it takes users to recreate a relevant sitemap or navigational menu.
- **Subjective satisfaction**: Ease of finding information, enjoyment of experience, how fresh or tired visitors feel after reading information and completing tasks.

To pass Nielsen's readability test, you want to write concise, focused, non-promotional copy. You also want to make it as easy as possible to scan, using various techniques we will discuss in detail in this chapter.

The passage on below, from my website, uses bullet points to make the text easy to scan. It also uses <u>hot links</u> that readers can click on if they want more information. This cuts down the overall copy volume by letting people who want more information on a particular topic to simply click on a relevant link.

> Based in Toronto, Paul Lima has been a <u>freelance writer,</u> <u>copywriter,</u> and <u>business-writing instructor</u> for over 25 years. He offers companies and organizations a variety of <u>business writing</u> and <u>copywriting</u> services and <u>business-writing training seminars.</u>
> - <u>Business Writing</u> - Case studies, copywriting (brochures, sales letter, and other promotional material), web content, media releases, proposals and reports
> - <u>Business Training</u> - Business writing, media interview preparation
> - <u>Writing Books</u> - Business writing, Media Release writing, Copywriting...
> - <u>For Freelancers</u> - Seminars, e-courses, books/e-books, writer's blog

But is it too concise?

If you don't want to use bullet points, you can still write easily scannable text. Simply use fewer words and simpler sentences:

> Based in Toronto, Paul has been a writer and writing instructor for over 25 years. He offers writing services and writing and media interview training. He has written books on writing and offers freelance writers several services.

Even though the above passage eschews promotional writing and is easy to scan, one might argue that the passage is too concise—that it leaves out important details—and a manager or client would never approve it, or a reader would not react to it in the appropriate manner. It is your job to recognize that the more copy you include, and the less scannable you make it, the lower the readability or comprehension level will be. However, you also have to keep in mind your purpose, your reader, and (sometimes) the wishes of a manager or client. In others words, you might have to walk a fine line between content and scanability. But keep in mind, if the copy is too difficult to scan, it will not be read; you will not accomplish your purpose.

Hot-link advantage

There are a number of techniques you can use to help readers scan.

One thing you can do to reduce copy volume is to use hyperlinks—hot-link keywords and phrases. In other words, instead of explaining a concept within a paragraph, you hot-link it so readers who want more detail can click and be taken to a page where they can read more, or they can click on a link that causes a text box with information to pop up. This reduces word volume you use on the original page, making the copy easier to scan.

In short, hot links let you give people content options while more effectively managing copy volume. You can use hot-links to do the following:

- Shorten paragraphs and pages to improve readability
- Increase page download speeds
- Link to background information
- Link readers to external sites to demonstrate objectivity
- Connect visitors to detailed studies (such as PDF files), multimedia presentations, or other Web pages

The following passage from the Canadian Cancer Society website (March, 2006) uses a subhead (explained below) to capture the attention of readers who are interested in 2006 cancer research grants awarded in Ontario and links people to grants by city and type and to a complete list of the grants.

2006 Research Grants in Ontario

Cancer researchers in Ontario received $18.7 million from the Canadian Cancer Society in 2006. Thirty-eight new grants were awarded to researchers in <u>Hamilton</u>, <u>Kingston</u>, <u>London</u>, <u>Ottawa</u>, and <u>Toronto</u> for promising research in several areas, including <u>skin cancer prevention</u> and <u>using viruses to stimulate a person's immune system</u> to fight cancer. Of the 72 new grants awarded across the country, 38 are going to Ontario researchers.

<u>View complete list of Canadian Cancer Society-funded research projects in Ontario.</u>

Hot-links can also be used to present different content at different levels to different audiences. For instance, not every person who reads the copy on testicular self-examination will want to perform a self-exam. The hot-linked text takes those readers who want to do so to a page where they can find out how. Notice, also, how other words and phrases in the passage are hot-linked to additional information, for those who want to know more about various aspects of this disease.

> Performing <u>testicular self-examination</u> (TSE) regularly helps you learn <u>what is normal</u> for your testicles so that you will be able to notice changes. See your doctor if you <u>notice</u> <u>anything unusual</u>.
>
> <u>Click here to learn how to perform a self-examination.</u>

Format fonts and subheads

To draw a reader's eye through a passage, you can use **bold type**, *italicized type*, <u>underlined type</u>, or color variations. However, I caution against excess use of these techniques, as well as against use of multiple typefaces (also known as typestyles or fonts) and type sizes, because a variety formats, fonts, and sizes can be distracting and even misleading. For instance, website readers often expect text that is a formatted differently to be hot linked, and they might click on your formatted text expecting to be taken to another page. However, if you use such variations judiciously, they can be an effective way to help your readers scan.

One effective way to use text variations to help readers scan is to use *meaningful* subheadings. Notice the emphasis on meaningful. Web readers want meaningful, not clever, information. When it comes to the use of headlines and subheads, they want copy that says, "Hey, this is about *x*, which is something you are interested in; otherwise, you would not have used *x* in your Google search."

If you review the pages of this book, you will see that I frequently use meaningful subheads. Occasionally, I use clever ones (or ones that I think are clever). I could use subheads more frequently and I could eliminate my attempts at being clever. However, you are a captive audience, one that has purchased this book and has a sense of purpose that this book is supposed to help you fill. That does not mean I should make this book difficult to read; it does mean that I can get away with a few more liberties than I would otherwise use on the Web.

Other techniques to assist scanning

Inverted pyramid. The inverted pyramid packs the most pertinent who, what, where, when, why, and sometimes how information into the opening paragraph or two of an article, as in this example from the *New York Times* (April 13, 2010):

> Two Democratic state lawmakers have sponsored a bill that would give principals in New York City the power to choose who should lose their jobs if the city needs to lay off teachers because of budget cuts, contradicting the current law under which teachers who have been in the system for the shortest amount of time would be the first to lose their jobs.

Take a moment and review the W5:

- *Who?* Two Democratic state lawmakers.
- *What?* Have sponsored a bill that would give principals in New York City the power to choose who should lose their jobs.
- *Where?* New York.
- *When?* Yesterday is implied; this news article was published the day after the bill was sponsored.
- *Why?* If the city needs to lay off teachers because of budget cuts.

Since most website visitors read the first paragraph or two before deciding if they will read on or not (some studies indicate *read/don't read* decisions are made even more quickly), packing the W5 into the opening paragraph ensures the reader sees the most important information you want to convey.

One idea per paragraph. To make it easier for readers to scan, try to use no more than one idea per paragraph. This will help you keep your paragraphs short, which will create more white space and make the document look easier to read. That psychology (that the page is easy to read) is important.

Bullet or numbered lists. As we have discussed, bullet (or numbered) passages are easier to scan than full block paragraphs.

Use fewer words. If you take the W5 approach, you can say a lot in very few words. Even if you have a lot to say, ask yourself if some readers only need a synopsis or summary—like an executive summary in a formal report. Combine the synopsis or summary with the power of the hot-link to offer readers who want more information the opportunity to click to read more.

Web writing in action

An April 27, 2009, online article written by Jakob Nielsen (see Alertbox at www.useit.com/alertbox) demonstrates how BBC News effectively harnesses the power of writing for the Web.

Notice how the article starts with a summary. Even though Web writing should be particularly concise and brief, Nielsen presents a summary to help readers decide, based on their objectives, if the article is worth reading. In addition, he uses hyperlinks to keep the article short. If the reader is particularly interested in a section that contains a hyperlink, the reader can click. Otherwise, the reader can read on.

He also uses bullet points to make the article scannable. Notice in particular how he combines bold type and bullet points. He bolds the first part of the bullet point because studies show many readers do not even read to the end of a line when scanning Web copy. In addition, he uses bold type judiciously part way through some lines. This technique pulls the reader's eye through the point because the eye sees the bold and the brain thinks: This could be important; I'd better go there.

Having said that about how Nielsen writes effectively for the Web, I want to restate that the article (on the next page) is about how the BBC News effectively harnesses the power of writing for the Web.

World's Best Headlines: BBC News

Summary:
Precise communication in a handful of words? The editors at BBC News achieve it every day, offering remarkable headline usability.

It's hard enough to <u>write for the Web</u> and meet the guidelines for <u>concise, scannable, and objective content</u>. It's *even harder* to write Web headlines, which must be:

- **short** (because people don't read much online);
- **rich in information scent**, clearly summarizing the target article;
- **front-loaded** with the most important keywords (because users often <u>scan only the beginning</u> of list items);
- **understandable out of context** (because headlines often appear without articles, as in search engine results); and
- **predictable**, so users know whether they'll like the full article before they click (because people don't return to sites that promise more than they deliver).

For several years, I've been impressed with BBC News headlines, both on the main BBC home page and on its dedicated <u>news page</u>. Most sites routinely violate headline guidelines, but BBC editors consistently do an awesome job.

Concise and Informative

On a recent visit, the BBC list of headlines for "other top stories" read as follows:

- Italy buries first quake victims
- Romania blamed over Moldova riots
- Ten arrested in UK anti-terrorism raids
- Villagers hurt in West Bank clash
- Mass Thai protest over leadership
- Iran accuses journalist of spying

Around the world in 38 words

The average headline consumed a mere **5 words** and **34 characters**. The amount of meaning they squeezed into this brief space is incredible: every word works hard for its living. I'm rarely that concise.

Each headline conveys the gist of the story on its own, without requiring you to click. Even better, each gives you a good idea of what you'll get if you do click and lets you judge—with a high degree of confidence—whether you'll be interested in the full article. As a result, you won't **waste clicks**. You'll click through to exactly those news items you want to read.

- Jakob Nielsen's Alertbox, April 27, 2009 (www.useit.com/alertbox)

Why concise Web writing?

You should have a solid understanding of the need for concise, easy-to-read Web writing. If you need this concept reinforced, think of website visitors as being engaged in hit-and-run information retrieval. They look at websites in this manner:

- Is the site interesting? If so,
  - Click
  - Retrieve
  - Move on
- If not,
  - Move on

It is your job to accommodate hit-and-run visitors. To do so, you have to use the techniques outlined above. However, you will also want to go beyond that. You also want to do the following:

- Use plain language readers understand
- Present chunks or screen-sized passages of text that convey your purpose and help your audience do what they want to do (or you want them to do) on your site

Unless you are simply archiving documents (a legitimate purpose) on your website, chunking and hyper-linking should work together to serve three purposes:

- Orient the reader
- Inform the reader
- Invite or motivate the reader to act

To orient the reader, the first part of any copy should let the reader know what the website (or specific page) is about. The page itself should be organized in a way that is easy to navigate, and each page on the site should have a consistent navigation (or menu) structure. Navigation menus go beyond the scope of this book because they are more of a design element; however, the writer might have to come up with names for various menu items or links. The names should be meaningful and speak to your visitor.

Web writing in action

Although the home page of my website (www.paullima.com) is not perfect, I'd like to think it embodies most of the writing-for-the-Web principles espoused here.

The page starts with my image, which may be its major flaw, and my slogan, which I hope captures the attention of the site visitor. Below my slogan is the primary menu, taking visitors to my most important pages. What then follows is a brief description about me and my services. Notice the hot-links in the description, making it easy for visitors who know what they want to click on the appropriate page.

freelance writer/writing trainer
media relations/interview consultant
freelance writer/writing trainer
media relations/interview consultant

paul lima: the right words. on time. on budget.

About | Contact | Business Writing | Business Training

Based in Toronto, business writer and business writing trainer Paul Lima can deliver the right words, on time and on budget, or train your staff to write more effectively. Paul has been a professional writer and writing instructor for over 25 years. He offers companies and organizations a variety of writing and editing services and business writing training.

- **Business Writing & Editing** - Case studies, copywriting (brochures and other sales and promotional material), web content, media releases
- **Business Training** - Business writing (email, reports, copywriting and sales material, web writing, speeches & presentations), media interview preparation, writing e-courses
- **Business Books** - *How to Write Media Releases, Copywriting that Works, How to Write a Non-fiction Book in 60 Days...*
- **For Freelancers** - e-courses, seminars, freelance writer's blog, books for writers

Contact | Business Writing | Business Training | Media Interview Training | Books |
| Writers Resources | Sample News Articles | Creative Writing | Site Map | Blog

Then there is a series of bullet point hot-links with short descriptions of what people will find if they click on the links. Finally, there is a more detailed navigational menu at the bottom of the site.

In short, when you visit my home page (as illustrated above), you see concise, focused copy that is easy to scan, and you are given four ways of getting to the most important inside pages.

Finally, when writing for the Web, if you have a media release, a report, or any other long document that you want to share with website visitors, you do not have to rewrite it for the Web. In other words, you can post print-based documents and material on a website as Adobe Acrobat PDF files or even as long website pages. However, you don't want to use such documents as your home page or a product or service feature page.

What you can do is link to print-based documents (such as PDFs) from an appropriate website page. Consider writing a summary or abstract of the document so the readers have more detail about what they are clicking through to. And, since this is the Web, expect some readers to read the summary and move on. If the summary is well written, the readers just might get all they need. However, if the document is critical and you really want it read, consider creating a Web-friendly version of it to help your website visitors read it.

Chapter 22: Direct Response Marketing

Note: This chapter on direct response marketing (DRM) sets the stage for writing website landing pages (pages you direct people to through online or offline advertising), which we cover later in the book. (You can read more information about advertising copywriting in my book, *Copywriting That Works: Bright Ideas to Help You Inform, Persuade, Motivate and Sell!*)

The communication process

Before we look at DRM (marketing meant to quickly solicit an immediate action or direct response), online ads, and website landing pages, I want to review the communication process introduced in Chapter 1 of this book.

As we have learned, communication requires a sender who sends a message through a channel to a receiver. However, the process is not complete without feedback, which closes the communication loop. Businesses that advertise want feedback so they can measure the effectiveness of online and offline DRM promotions. The method used to solicit feedback often changes based on the medium and the purpose of the message.

For instance, an advertiser who wants to solicit feedback based on an ad that is meant to raise brand awareness might survey a segment of the target market before and after the ad runs to determine if the ad has raised awareness. An advertiser interested in sales may look at sales and store traffic on the day the ad runs, and for a few days afterwards. An online business is able to track traffic or click-throughs generated by various online promotions. Ideally, the company should set up various Web pages or landing pages to measure hits from each form of advertising used.

In DRM, the advertiser wants to solicit immediate feedback (response) directly from the message receiver. For instance, if an advertiser sends an electronic newsletter to an e-mail list, the advertising might request that readers click on a link to a website. Count the clicks, and you have feedback on your request. An advertiser who sends a direct mail flyer to a mailing list might ask recipients to call a toll-free number and enter a specific code to receive more information. Count the calls, and you have feedback.

In other words, if the purpose of the e-mail ad is to motivate an action such as visiting a website, then click-throughs from the e-mail to the website, which can be automatically measured, constitute feedback. If the purpose is to get the audience to call for more information, then calls for more information constitute feedback.

Gauging versus motivating

When it comes to direct mail, motivating action that can be gauged is paramount. Gauging feedback is important; however, if you do not motivate action, you will have little feedback to gauge. Which begs the question: how do you motivate action, such as a sale?

When you gauge sales, you find ways of relating sales to the ad. For instance, you might look at sales results on the day before, the day of, and the day after a newspaper ad ran. When you motivate sales, you use incentives to motivate people to give you feedback (take action such as buy something). Before you can motivate action, you have to capture attention, maintain interest, and influence attitude, as we have said.

If you want action, it is your job to define the action you want and then to motivate it—to give your target market an incentive to act. A simple method of motivating action is to include a coupon in an ad—something like a "buy one bag of potato chips get a second bag free" coupon. The advertiser might do this to introduce a new brand of chips. An online software advertiser might create a banner ad or Google ad that mentions a thirty-day free trial offer.

To be effective, DRM print ads or brochures must include all the information necessary to lead the prospect directly to an action. Online DRM ads tend to focus on motivating readers to click. The click takes the reader to a website landing page where they can read information that, in theory, motivates them to take the next step—buy the product, request a callback from a sales representative, donate to a charity, support a cause, and so on. The DRM call to action frequently includes incentives to motivate the target market to act.

Hook, line, and sinker

To capture attention, hold interest, influence attitude, and motivate readers to act, the DRM ad uses the hook, line, and sinker approach to marketing.

Hook. To hook the target market, the advertiser uses various landmark words with which the target market can identify. Often, in business-to-consumer DRM, the job of the writer is to capture attention (hook the reader) by creating desire and promising fulfillment. In business-to-business DRM, however, the job of the writer is to hook the reader by identifying a problem and offering a solution.

Line. The body copy, or line, reinforces how the product or service solves the problem, fills the need, or satisfies the desire. It also builds trust by reassuring the client through guarantees and testimonials. And it anticipates and overcomes objections because people will not act if they have objections. In short, the body copy or line presents information—such as price, guarantees, return policy, and so on—the target market needs before they will take action.

Sinker. This is the call to action. It tells readers what the advertiser wants them to do, how to do it, where to do it, and when to do it by. And it generally uses a time-limited offer (incentive) to motivate the reader to buy the product, visit a website, call for a demo, make an appointment with a sales representative, fill out a survey that further qualifies the target market, and so forth. The hook can actually contain the incentive or allude to it in some way as a kind of teaser that motivates the reader to read.

Focus on the prospect, not the product

Before writing business-to-business DRM material, the most useful background research you can do is to ask your typical prospect: "What's the biggest problem or opportunity you have right now?" By ensuring the copy answers that question, you focus on the needs of the prospect. Of course, you will tie that answer into the features and benefits of the product or service you are selling, but you will put the prospect first.

That can also be the case in business-to-consumer DRM. Ideally, your copy focuses on the greatest desire or aspiration of the target market. However, you can still think of it in terms of problem/solution. If the target market cannot achieve his or her desires and aspirations, the target market has a problem. And that, for the advertiser, is an opportunity to offer a solution in the hook.

DRM writing process

There are several steps you should take before writing a DRM brochure or website landing page, such as defining or determining the following:

- Sales/marketing objective or purpose
- Target market demographics
- Target market's issue, problem, opportunity, need, or desire
- Target market's objections
- Specific objection you must overcome
- How to overcome them
- How to build trust
- Your call to action
- Incentive to motivate action

Again, if you are creating an online ad meant to motivate a click (the response), you will not address all those points, as we shall see when we examine Google ads. However, you still have to capture attention and motivate action—the click. No small order, that. Once readers click, they land on the landing page—the page that covers all the points outlined above to help the reader make a buy (or no buy) decision.

Chapter 23: Writing Short Web Ads

When it comes to writing for the Web, writing Google ads is about as short as it gets. If you go to Google and search for "Google ads," you'll find about 50,900,000 Google search engine links. It does not cost anything to have a Web page indexed in the Google. However, if my website had information about Google ads and it was ranked one million links down, visitors would never find my site. To combat a low rank, I can set up an ad on Google using Google AdWords:

Top Website Advertising
Get your Website found on 1st page.
Get Your $80 Free Advertising Now!
www.INeedHits.com/web-advertising

This particular ad was listed number one (results are subject to change) when I used the search term "Google ads." How did the advertiser manage to get the ad listed first? He used Google AdWords to set up the ad to show up when Google visitors search for keywords related to Google ads and he paid more per click than others who associated similar ads with keywords related to Google ads.

With AdWords, you create your own ad, choose keywords to help Google match your ad to your audience, and pay only when someone clicks on your ad. The more you're willing to pay and the more times people click on your ad, the higher your ad ranks. Since rank for Google ads is a combination of the price you pay and how popular your ad is based on clicks, your copy had better be effective enough to encourage clicks.

Let me repeat that: *Your copy had better be effective enough to encourage clicks.* When you place an ad on Google, you want a response—a click. In short, Google ads are four-line DRM ads.

AdWords character (letters, symbols, spaces) limitations are strict. You cannot go over character count when you create your headline, two lines of text, and your display URL. Here are the maximum character counts:

- **Headline**: 25 characters
- **Line 1**: 35 characters
- **Line 2**: 35 characters
- **Display URL**: 35 characters

Writing Google ads

When we look more closely at the number-one ranked ad based on the search term "Google ads" we see the following:

1. Hook or attention-grabbing headline: "Top Website Advertising"
2. Line or interest-holding body copy: "Get your Website found on 1st page"
3. Sinker or incentive meant to motivate the click: "Get Your $80 Free Advertising Now!"

Now let's go to Google and search for something computer-oriented: contact management software. Let's look at one of the software ads:

Contact Mgt Software
Fully integrated with Outlook.
30-day free trial.
www.NetSuite.com

Isn't that headline boring? All it does is repeat the keywords. But wait a minute! What was I looking for? Does that headline not tell me that I have found exactly what I was looking for? If I use Outlook, as most businesses do, I'm interested. And there's a free trial. What have I got to lose? Click. And I'm on the landing page, the page that then tries to sell me. (We'll look at landing page copy in the next chapter.)

In summary, you can pack a lot into a few short lines—including a hook, line, and sinker. And in many ways, that's what writing for the Web is all about—saying as much as you can in as few words as possible. But not using so few words that your readers miss your point or purpose and do not know what you want them to do. Keep that in mind as you are writing Web-based copy, or pretty much any copy for that matter.

Chapter 24: Website Landing Pages

When it comes to DRM and the Web, all the rules apply—more or less. On the Web, prospects often find you using search engines. They enter key-words related to your product or service and up pops a link and/or ad related to your website. The searcher, who has prequalified himself or herself by entering keywords related to your product, service, or cause, clicks on the link and lands on your home page or any other page you have optimized to show up in a search engine based on specific search terms.

If the searcher clicks on a Google ad, the ad should take the prospect to a landing page—your online DRM page—not to your website home page. What's the difference between a home page and a landing page? A home page has a Web address such as www.yoursite.com and generally includes links to all the main pages on a website. A landing page might have a Web address such as www.yoursite.com/product-info and is set up to solicit a direct response from a prospect who lands on it after clicking on a link.

In short, a landing page is a Web page that users click to from an online ad. Landing pages are used by advertisers who wish to provide a special offer in response to a click-through on a search engine link, banner ad, or pay-per-click (PPC) ad. For best results, landing pages should be highly targeted to the person who might click on the ad, and are set up using DRM principles.

Although a landing page does not have to include all the elements that a DRM brochure requires, a landing page can offer much more information than most DRM brochures because it has what is called "the hot-link advantage." The hot link advantage lets you incorporate links on your landing page so visitors can click on them for more information. For instance, you can create a link from the landing page to the full list of features and benefits, or to the complete details of your guarantee.

Having said that, some advertisers believe you should put everything you want to say about your product or service on the landing page itself. This makes for longer landing pages and is often used in business-to-consumer sales. Whether you include all the copy required to close the sale on the landing page or on the landing page and on various hot-linked pages (a debate that can left for another book), you still need a hook, line, and sinker. However, the first thing you need is a call to action, perhaps in conjunction with a sinker.

Why a call to action first? Think about it. Landing page visitors are hot prospects. They pre-qualified themselves by using keywords related to your product and clicked on a Google ad or search engine link about your product. Why wouldn't you offer such visitors a way to buy—a link that says "Buy Now!" or at least "Try Now!" (if you are selling software, for instance)? If the visitors are hot prospects, they can buy right away. If they are just curious, they can continue to read your landing page copy.

Busy as a bee

On the next page is the landing page for U-Rent-It Manager (URIM), a party/event rental and small equipment rental order-entry and reservation software system. (The application is real; the name has been changed.)

If you have ever rented equipment or tools, you probably feel lucky if the reserved equipment is there when you show up. The equipment rental staff is running around like chickens with their heads cut off and you wonder if they actually know what they is doing. The folks are busy, no doubt about it. But are they organized?

The U-Rent-It Manager application claims it will organize inventory and staff so that rental customers get the products they have reserved. URIM has a Google AdWords campaign. The ads take the prospect to the URIM landing page where the first thing visitors see is a link to a thirty-day free trial offer for the application. Click on the link and you see guarantees and other trust-building copy, as well as a link to the terms and conditions (kept as simple as possible) and, of course, the download link.

The sales offer is put up front because visitors have prequalified themselves by using keywords to search for such a product and just might want to buy it. So why not make it easy to buy, or at least try? (Layout and design are important to make the page easy to read and the requested action easy to follow.)

But what if the visitor still needs convincing? The landing page contains sales and promotional copy as well. Notice the use of bullet points in the sample copy. As discussed, they make copy easy to scan. Often the designer will indicate where bullet points should be placed, but the copywriter can also make the suggestion. Here is URIM's landing page copy:

Busy as a bee? But are you as efficient?

- Get everyone in your hive working together
- Take the guesswork out of inventory tracking and planning
- Eliminate recopying and re-keying orders
- Deliver the right product to the right client, at the right time
- Spend more time growing your business!

The beehive may look like a chaotic site, but it is efficiency in motion. U-Rent-It Manager (URIM) is a party/event rental and small equipment rental order-entry and reservation system that can bring beehive efficiency to your business.

With online inventory tracking, and sales and order calculations, URIM will have you buzzing with excitement.

Remove the guesswork

URIM takes the guesswork out of inventory tracking and planning and eliminates the need to recopy or re-enter orders. URIM includes contact manager and marketing functions and a "one-button click" to export accounting data to QuickBooks.

URIM is a cost-effective way to combat chaos and introduce order to your rental business. It saves you time and makes your hive a more productive place.

Designed with valuable input from the party/event and small equipment rental industry, and fully supported by phone, e-mail, and online support, URIM is an intuitive application that will have you seeing positive results in a few hours.

Right product, right person, right time

Get the right product to the right person at the right time. Generate increased customer satisfaction and repeat business. Create more time to expand your business. Produce more honey. Now that's sweet!

Hive in Action: URIM Features and Benefits

Free Taste of Rental Manager: Download Demo

Build Your Hive: Purchase URIM

Notice the hot links at the end of the landing page copy. If readers want to know more, they can click on features and benefits. If they want to try the product at no charge, they can. If they want to buy, they can do that too. On the demo page, prospects find guarantees and other trust-building copy. On all the pages, they find links back to the landing page and links to all the other pages.

Here is some copy from Hive in Action: URIM Features and Benefits page:

Transform your business into a hive of productivity

"When I finally decided to update my 20-year-old 'computerized' system, I went looking for a cost-efficient, integrated rental order-entry and reservation system from a supplier who was readily available for support, if I needed it. I have found all this with URIM."
- Gord Robinson, WeRentIt

With URIM in place, your business will still be a hive of activity. But all activity will be focused on meeting and exceeding customer expectations, generating repeat business, and growing your business. Use URIM to:

- Become more organized and productive, better manage workload, and keep the customer satisfied
- Reserve inventory for specific time periods
- Receive alerts if you are about to over-book items
- Reserve any special equipment needed for set up
- Produce quotes without reserving inventory
- Convert quotes into orders with a "one-button click"
- Enter separate billing and shipping addresses on forms
- Confirm and send quotes and orders by e-mail
- Print delivery and pick-up forms to expedite delivery
- Better manage receivables and analyze sales
- Include tax exemptions and discounts on invoices
- Calculate overall sales automatically

Free Taste of Rental Manager: Download Demo
Build Your Hive: Purchase URIM
URIM: Getting Started [**Note**: Takes reader to landing page]

In short, the kind of thinking that you put into your print DRM material goes into your Web-based DRM landing page:

- What do people need to know before they take the action that you want them to take?
- How can you build trust and confidence?
- What kind of incentive can you offer to entice them to take action while they are on the site?

When you write for the Web, you want to make it as easy as possible for readers to scan and absorb your copy. That means writing shorter sentences and paragraphs, using bold headers and bullet points when and where appropriate. (These same principles can be applied to print-based DRM brochures as well.)

Let's look at part of another landing page, below, for media interview training. It puts a call to action for a free report close to the top of the page. This is a common landing page tactic. The free report includes practical information the reader can use, more information about the training offered, and contact information. The free report call to action on the landing page does not interfere with the overall flow of the copy (again, design and layout is as critical as the writing of copy here). Of course, the free offer is repeated at the end of the landing page as well, along with relevant contact information.

Are you ready for your interview?

You never know when a reporter will call. So be prepared. Paul Lima can have you ready in one interactive session.

Are you seeking media attention? Are journalists seeking you? Either way, you need to be prepared for interviews with journalists, because they are prepared to interview you.

Why be prepared?

It's the information age and every executive, manager, corporate spokesperson, and business owner should be able to condense news, financial data, product information, and other announcements into brief, convincing messages—expressed in an articulate, memorable manner.

When it comes to getting your organization's message out to the public—customers, shareholders, sponsors, donors, and other stakeholders—knowing how to talk to journalists and interact effectively with the media is essential. What you say and how you say it can have a lasting impact on your business because the media helps Canadians form opinions.

> **Request your FREE** *Are You Ready for Your Interview* report today. The report gives you practical advice to help you prepare for interviews with print and broadcast reporters. E-mail: info@paullima.com with "Media Interview Report" in the subject line.

The key to successful interviews?

Developing and delivering a message that is simple, interesting, and newsy is key to successful interviews. In most interviews, you should stick to several carefully crafted key messages and draw on a couple supporting points and examples. You should judiciously repeat key messages for emphasis, while answering questions. Paul Lima's half-day or full-day media interview training seminars will show you how to do just that.

> *"We have been using Paul Lima for media training for every client at Infinity PR. Paul's training is insightful and our clients take away great learning from the sessions. All of our clients have been extremely happy with the training."* - Alan McLaren, Infinity PR

The landing page copy goes on to describe how the media training seminars can help you prepare for media interviews in one interactive session, in person or over the phone (which is how many interviews are conducted), and describes the learning objectives of the training. It also includes another testimonial, a link to an article that describes how media interview training, coupled with effective PR, turned a book into a Canadian bestseller, and contact information. Finally, it repeats the "request your free media interview training report" information.

Again, this approach puts a call to action up front. The use of bold subheads, short paragraphs, and boxes for the testimonials all make the copy easy to scan. There is no incentive to "buy" media training; however, the call to action for the free report is clearly stated, as is the contact information. The free report would be used to demonstrate the trainer's knowledge about media interviews and would include contact information and a call to action.

In summary, when writing for the Web, you want copy that:

- Is clear, concise, focused, well written, and easy to scan and absorb;
- Speaks to a clearly defined target market;
- Conveys your purpose and supports your purpose; and
- Presents a clear call to action and, if appropriate, an incentive to act.

Generally, Web copy should be more concise and shorter than print-based writing; however, you still need to capture attention, hold interest, influence attitude, and ask for action. In short, Web copy should not be so short that it skips any of those steps. It should also not be so concise that it leaves out important information that the reader requires before deciding to act.

Again, if you have a media release, a report, or any other long document that you want to share with website visitors, you do not have to rewrite it or format it for the Web. You can post it on your website and link to it. If your site visitors need to read it, they will. But it's a good idea to include a summary of the document with your link to inform the reader about the document topic and purpose. That will help readers decide if they wants to click and read. However, if the document is critical, consider creating a Web-friendly version of it to help site visitors read it.

Chapter 25: Mission/Vision Statements

We are moving back to print copy, although many companies also link to their mission statements on their websites. So if you ever have to write a mission statement, or work in collaboration on one, find out where it will run; write, or at least format, for that medium.

Most companies and organizations have mission statements. They often delegate the task of writing them to employee groups of, or lead by, senior executives. On the other hand, various departments tend to contribute to the business plan through a formal process. The contributions are then pieced together by one person who also edits them for consistency.

Mission statements

Business plans typically start with mission statements. A mission statement serves as a road map that helps an organization determine the direction it wants to go. Some mission statements are a line long or a couple of sentences long. However, many mission statements run for several paragraphs and include the following components:

- Purpose and aim of the organization
- Organization's primary stakeholders
- Responsibilities of the organization toward stakeholders
- Products and services offered

In other words, mission statements generally paint the strategic objective of the company by describing what the company offers, why, and to whom. The stakeholders can include employees, customers, the larger community, and perhaps others. I confess that I often find long, convoluted mission statements to be a tad on the dull side, but they can serve an important purpose for many companies. I am partial to short mission statements that work to focus a business.

Here is the mission statement for my business:

> To deliver the right words, on time and on budget. Or to train individuals to deliver the right words, on time and on budget.

In other words, I write effectively and efficiently for companies or I train their people to do so. If you ask me to design your flyer or website, I'll look at my mission statement and say, "Sorry, I don't do that." If you ask me to plan and coordinate a PR event, you'll get the same answer. I can write your media release, but not plan and coordinate your event. (As an aside, I will help clients find someone who can do that work and hope my involvement in finding that person helps me pick up some of the writing work.)

The best mission statements are written using plain language, with no technical jargon and no adornment. Like the mission statement of the International Red Cross—"To serve the most vulnerable"—they come right out and say something clear, concise, and focused. In their brevity and simplicity is power.

Here are several other mission statements:

- 3M: "To solve unsolved problems innovatively."
- Mary Kay Cosmetics: "To give unlimited opportunity to women."
- Intel Corporation: "Delight our customers, employees, and shareholders by relentlessly delivering the platform and technology advancements that become essential to the way we work and live."
- An investigative reporter I know: "Agitate. Agitate."

The Intel mission statement is simple and straight-forward, especially when you consider how large Intel is. Often, short mission statements are supported by a set of values that direct the implementation of the mission. Intel states its values as follows:

- Customer orientation
- Results orientation
- Risk taking
- Great place to work
- Quality
- Discipline

Many believe that mission statements should have a grand scale, be socially meaningful, and be measurable. The following historical mission statements are grand in scale but still simple in scope as far as the writing is concerned:

- Ford Motor Company (early 1900s): "Ford will democratize the automobile."
- Sony (early 1950s): "Become the company most known for changing the worldwide poor-quality image of Japanese products."
- Boeing (1950): "Become the dominant player in commercial aircraft and bring the world into the jet age."

Although one-line mission statements are admirable, there are times when the author's purpose requires the writing of more than one line. For example, you would use a longer mission statement when submitting a business plan to a bank as part of a request for financing. But whether a mission statement is one line or several paragraphs, it should always speak clearly to all stakeholders and convey its message in a concise, focused manner.

Vision statement

I want to move for a moment from mission statements to vision statements. A vision statement tends to be more focused on the immediate future. For instance, *democratizing the automobile* and *becoming a $125 billion company* are big picture missions. Vision statements tend to look at what a company must do over the next year to take a step toward fulfilling its mission. (To complicate matters, some companies have a more immediately focused mission statement and a broader-based vision statement. But now we are dealing with semantics.)

Before you work on either one, clarify the purpose of the document you are writing. (Sound familiar?) To do that, you might want to ask the *why* question:

Why am I writing this?

Armed with the answer, and the knowledge of where the mission or vision statement will appear and who will read it, you should be able to write a concise and focused mission or vision statement.

Although my mission drives my business in terms of the big picture—*I write and train*—my vision drives me. It is who I see (envision) myself as. To write it, I use the five Ws: who, what, where, when, and why. Allow me to show you how I use the five Ws to help me write my business vision.

Paul Lima's Business Vision

Who: Paul Lima is a business writer, writing instructor, and media interview trainer. He writes for companies in the technology, telecom, financial services, printing, consumer goods and other sectors, and trains executives and employees in various sectors.

What: Writes/edits case studies, media releases, ad copy, direct mail brochure copy, advertorials, Google ads, website landing pages, and white papers for corporate clients. Conducts business writing, copywriting and media interview training seminars for corporate clients.

Where: He writes at his home office and conducts training at client locations. He travels mostly within the Greater Toronto Area. He is not seeking contract employment that would require him to work daily in an office.

When: He works Monday to Friday (business hours) and conducts occasional evening and weekend workshops.

Why: He loves it. After fifteen years of working full-time, he chose to work from home as a freelancer. After ten years of freelance writing, he chose to conduct training to add greater variety to his workload.

This vision statement reminds me that I chose this business and that this is what I want to do. It is not forward looking (again, some vision statements pronounce where the company or organization will be in five or ten years); however, I review it every year so that I can, if necessary, adjust my vision of me—Paul Lima, the businessperson. I have seen a number of forward-looking vision statements—this is what we are, this is what we want to be, this is when we want to be it—and I like how they keep the business on track. There is nothing wrong, and a lot right, with having a dream and following it.

For me though, the vision statement, much more than the mission statement, drives my business and marketing plans. I mention marketing plan here because, to me, the marketing plan is an important component of the business plan. It is so important that many companies produce marketing plans based on, but separate from, their business plans.

Business plan overview

The business plan is the vehicle that gets the organization where it wants to go. Just as a vehicle is more complex than a road map, a business plan is much longer than a mission statement and includes many more components.

For most companies, the business plan says, "This is who we are, what we do, who we do it for, how we do it, and this is what we are going to make happen and how we are going to make it happen." In short, anyone reading it would know what business the company is in and would know what the company hopes to accomplish that year. But not many people would read it, unless the company was looking for investment capital or communicating a change of direction to employees.

For the most part, business plans tend to be internal documents that executives can review monthly or quarterly (along with sales and financial statements) to help them determine if the company is on track, or not.

Start-up companies and mature companies that want to grow dynamically often seek financing from banks, private investors, or the stock market. Business plans for such companies are more like proposals. They detail everything in a business plan that will be made public—or at least shown to potential investors. Such plans are more forward looking and talk about strategic opportunities and competitive advantages. In short, such a plan tells potential investors where the company is now and where it plans to be in five or ten years, how it plans on getting there, and what rate of return investors can expect. (Publicly traded companies have to adhere to a number of rules and regulations when making forward-looking statements, a discussion of which is outside the scope of this book.)

Either way, business plans tend to include the following sections:
- Company legal name and incorporation details
- Company description and big picture strategy
- Financial goals and objectives

- Management team and descriptions
- Financial analysis—strengths and/or investment requirements
- Supporting documents, such as market research data, audited financial statements, and so on
- Products and/or services offered and anything else the company does
- Growth opportunity of each product or service offering
- Products and/or services under development
- Market analysis or opportunity
- Marketing plan
- Mission and/or vision statement (in most business plans, this information appears in the first section in the document, after the title page, executive summary, and table of contents)

Before you write

Before you write a business plan, you should consider the points below.

Know your purpose: Are you seeking a bank loan, looking to raise private capital, hoping to take your company public, trying to boost sales and revenue, or combating increased competition? Your purpose, as I hope we have seen throughout this book, drives your tone and content.

Produced mission and vision statements first. The mission statement and vision statement are your road map. Don't start this journey without your road map in place or you will get lost.

Include a marketing plan. (Detailed marketing plans go beyond the scope of this book.) As part of your business plan, the marketing plan is the *how* of your business plan. It is how you are going to do what you said you were going to do—how you are going to promote and sell your goods and/or services.

What now?

Now you take a stab at writing a mission statement and a business vision, and perhaps even a first draft of a business plan. Before you write, pick the company or organization you want to write about. Feel free to use any of the following as your starting point:

- The company you work for, even if you are not in a senior position
- A company you have worked for

- A school that you attend or attended
- A charity or not-for-profit association you do volunteer work for
- A business you are currently running or might one day like to run

Once you have in mind the company or organization you want to write about, think about your purpose. For example, are you trying to raise capital from bankers or trying to get all your employees to row in the same direction? Whatever your purpose is, jot it down to keep yourself focused. Think also about your audience: Who do you envision reading this? What's in it for the reader? Jot that down too.

Now do a little brainstorming. I suggest you try clustering and answering the W5 questions in point form. You might be able to write your mission statement and your business vision based on your W5 work and your clustering; however, before you write your business plan, create an outline. Use the business plan sections detailed above to help you organize your thoughts outline points. Once you have your outline in place, try a directed freefall. Freefall from outline point to outline point until you have completed the first draft of your business plan.

In short, follow the writing process, and you should do well.

And that's it. I hope you enjoyed the book. All the best with your writing. – Paul

About the Author

Based in Toronto, Canada, Paul Lima has been a professional writer and writing instructor for over 25 years. He has run a successful freelance writing and business-writing training business since 1988.

For corporate clients, Paul writes media releases, case studies, sales letters, direct-response brochures, website copy, and other material.

For newspapers and magazines, Paul writes about small business and technology issues. His articles have appeared in the *Globe and Mail, Toronto Star, National Post, Backbone, Profit*, CBC.ca, and many other publications.

As a qualified educator, Paul conducts seminars on business writing, media interview preparation, and freelance writing.

An English major from York University and a member of the Professional Writers Association of Canada, Paul has worked as an advertising copywriter, continuing education manager, and magazine editor.

Paul is the author of 10 books and 3 short e-reports, listed below. Read more about him online at www.paullima.com.

Books and short reports by Paul Lima:

- *Harness the Business Writing Process*
- *How to Write a Non-fiction Book in 60 Days*
- *(re)Discover the Joy of Creative Writing*
- *Everything You Wanted to Know About Freelance Writing*
- *The Six-Figure Freelancer: How to Find, Price and Manage Corporate Writing Assignments*
- *Business of Freelance Writing: How to Develop Article Ideas and Sell Them to Newspapers and Magazines*
- *Copywriting That Works: Bright ideas to Help You Inform, Persuade, Motivate and Sell!*

- *How to Write Media Releases to Promote Your Business, Organization or Event*
- *Do you Know Where Your Website Ranks? How to Optimize Your Website for the Best Possible Search Engine Results*
- *Build A Better Business Foundation: Create a Business Vision, Write a Business Plan, Produce a Marketing Plan*
- *If You Don't Know Where You are Going, How are You Going to Get There? Business Vision Short eReport*
- *Put Time On Your Side: Time Management Short eReport*
- *Are You Ready for Your Interview:* Free media interview training report

Available online through **www.paullima.com/books**

CPSIA information can be obtained at www.ICGtesting.com
Printed in the USA
LVOW030208130712

289831LV00021B/10/P